# Words Every 3rd Grader Needs to Know!

## By Lee S. Justice

**Frank Schaffer Publications**
An imprint of Carson-Dellosa Publishing LLC
Greensboro, North Carolina

# Table of Contents

Frank Schaffer Publications
An imprint of Carson-Dellosa Publishing LLC
PO Box 35665
Greensboro, NC 27425 USA

ISBN 978-0-76823-553-1
123107800

Dear Teacher,

Welcome to *Words Every Third Grader Needs to Know!* This vocabulary series supports and supplements instruction in the content areas. The reproducible pages are designed to give students extra practice in using academic vocabulary. Academic vocabulary includes the subject-specific words that often challenge learners—words such as *quotient*, *predator*, and *context clue*—which they rarely encounter in everyday use. Terms like these may be challenging, but they are also essential to a student's ability to learn new subject concepts.

The 200 words in *Words Every Third Grader Needs to Know!* have been selected to match national education standards in the curriculum areas. The activities feature the vocabulary words in a variety of contexts so that students can actively think about how each word is used and make their own thoughtful connections to them.

*Words Every Third Grader Needs to Know!* is organized by content area. Start with any content area you wish. Then, provide students with the activity pages in order. An **Introduction Page** starts each section. It features a list of the words in that section, with two blanks before each word. Have students use the rating scale to evaluate their knowledge of each word before they do the activities and then again after completing the activities. **Explore a Word** activities have students focus on one word at a time to create their own associations. **Compare Words** activities show students how two related words are alike and different in meaning. **Make Connections** activities help students understand the relationships among words that are often used together. And **Play With Words** activities provide additional context and review in a playful format.

Additional features appear on some of the activity pages. **Word Alert!** activities point out word concepts, including structural elements, such as prefixes and suffixes, and word families with shared roots. **Look It Up!** activities help students develop dictionary skills as they investigate multiple meanings, word origins, and more. And **Challenge!** activities are starting points to get students thinking critically.

The **Student Dictionary** pages are organized by content area and support the activity pages in each section. Students should use the Student Dictionary as they work on each activity page. You may also use the Student Dictionary to model and review dictionary skills, such as alphabetical order, pronunciation, and parts of speech. Each section of the Student Dictionary ends with space for students to write more words and meanings from their subject learning. Reinforce and extend vocabulary knowledge by using the **Game Ideas and Suggestions** section, which includes ideas for the word cards provided at the back of this book, and game templates intended for small group or whole group activities.

We believe that with *Words Every Third Grader Needs to Know!*, your students will be well equipped with the necessary skills for success with subject-specific vocabulary.

Sincerely,
Frank Schaffer Publications

# How to Use the Vocabulary Word Cards

Word cards with key vocabulary words are provided at the end of this book. These can be used as flash cards, also called *association cards*, to help students build quick associations between a word and its content-related meaning. Create additional word cards with all of the vocabulary words from this book or with additional words from your students' content-area learning. Incorporate the cards as you teach new vocabulary words. Use the cards to create a word wall. Or select one card and use that word for "Word of the Day" type activities. You can also use the cards for extension games and activities. Below are a few ideas to get you started.

 **Know, Don't Know**

Step 1: Student reads each word and definition in the pile.

Step 2: Student reads each word and tries to say its definition. If correct, the card goes in the "Know" pile. If incorrect, the card goes in the "Don't Know" pile.

Step 3: Student repeats Step 1, using only the "Don't Know" pile cards.

Step 4: Student repeats Step 2, and so on.

Step 5: After correctly defining each word in the original pile, the student tries again several days later.

 **Quiz Show**

Select a quizmaster to read each word or its definition to a panel of three contestants or to two teams of contestants. Each contestant or team has ten seconds to write the definition or the word. If they do so correctly, they earn a point. The winner has the most points at the end of a predetermined time period or number of words.

 **Guessing Game**

Display a selected group of cards, and play "I'm thinking of a word that. . . ." Offer students one clue at a time, including clues about word structure and relationships. Encourage students to raise their hands only when they are "absolutely sure" of the word.

Example for the word *explorer*:
- I'm thinking of a word that has to do with history.
- This word has a suffix that names someone who does something.
- This word is often used with *sailing ship*, *maps*, and *discovery*.
- This word tells who Christopher Columbus was.
- What's the word?

Encourage students to try their hand at offering clues.

# Important Math Words You Need to Know!

Use this list to keep track of how well you know the new words.

0 = Don't Know     1 = Know It Somewhat     2 = Know It Well

___ ___ angle

___ ___ area

___ ___ decimal point

___ ___ denominator

___ ___ diagonal

___ ___ digit

___ ___ division

___ ___ equilateral triangle

___ ___ fraction

___ ___ hexagon

___ ___ line segment

___ ___ measurement

___ ___ multiple

___ ___ multiplication

___ ___ numerator

___ ___ octagon

___ ___ pentagon

___ ___ perimeter

___ ___ perpendicular

___ ___ polygon

___ ___ product

___ ___ quotient

___ ___ rectangle

___ ___ remainder

___ ___ right triangle

# Explore a Word

Follow these steps.

**1.** Read the paragraph below. Think about the meaning of the **bold** term.

> In everyday language, the word *line* names something that looks like this: _____. But in the language of math, a line goes on in a straight path without an end. If the straight path has two endpoints, it is called a **line segment**.

**2.** What do you think the term means? Write your idea.

**line segment:** _____

_____

**3.** Write a sentence with the term **line segment**. Show what it means.

_____

_____

**4.** Check the meaning of **line segment** in the Student Dictionary.

**5.** If your sentence in step 3 matches the meaning, put a ✓ after it. If your sentence does not match the meaning, write a better sentence.

_____

_____

**6.** Make a simple drawing to show the meaning of **line segment**.

# Explore a Word

Read the sentence below. Think about the meaning of the **bold** word. Then, check the Student Dictionary.

> Take a **measurement** of your foot so that you choose the correct shoe size.

Fill out the web to show your ideas about measurement.

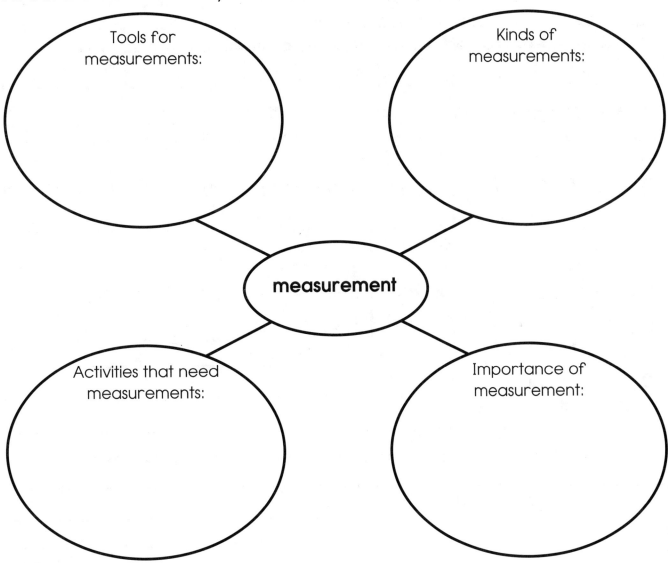

Tools for measurements:

Kinds of measurements:

**measurement**

Activities that need measurements:

Importance of measurement:

## 🔍 Word Alert!

A suffix is a word part added to the end a word. What suffix is added to the base word *measure* to form the vocabulary word on this page?

_____

_____

# Compare Words

Look at the picture and caption. Think about the meaning of each **bold** word. Then, check the Student Dictionary.

I inch

4 inches

Add the lengths of the sides. The **perimeter** is 10 inches.
Count the number of square units that fit inside. The **area** is 4 square inches.

Write the words *perimeter* and *area* where they fit in the sentences. Then, draw a picture with labels to show the measurements that are described.

1. We rode our bikes 4 miles on a path around the _____ of the park. The _____ of the park is 1 square mile.

2. One side of a square rug is 3 feet long. The _____ of the rug is 12 feet. The _____ of the rug is 9 square feet.

3. The _____ of the sheet of paper is 15 square inches. The _____ of the sheet is 16 inches.

# Compare Words

Look at the picture and labels. Think about the meaning of each **bold** word. Then, check the Student Dictionary.

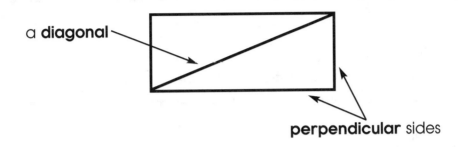

a **diagonal**

**perpendicular** sides

Circle the word that completes each sentence.

1. The floor and the wall are (diagonal/perpendicular) to each other.

2. Connect opposite corners with a (diagonal/perpendicular) line.

3. (Diagonal/Perpendicular) lines are slanted.

4. A square has sides that are (diagonal/perpendicular).

5. Two (diagonal/perpendicular) sides of the roof meet at the top.

Look around. What perpendicular things do you see? Where do you see diagonals? Write an example of each.

6. perpendicular: _____

7. diagonal: _____

# Make Connections

Read the example and sentence. Think about the meaning of each **bold** term. Then, check the Student Dictionary.

> $132.24
>
> The **digit** 2 stands for two dollars before the **decimal point**. To the right of the decimal point, the digit 2 stands for twenty cents.

Follow each instruction.

1. Write the digits 3, 5, and 7 in order. Circle the digit that is in the tens place.

   _____

2. Use numbers to write the amount ten dollars and fifty-two cents. Circle the decimal point.

   _____

3. Write a number in which the digit 6 stands for six tenths.

   _____

4. Do amounts become larger to the left of a decimal point, or do they become smaller? Explain your answer with an example.

   _____

 **Look It Up!**

The word *digit* has more than one meaning. Use a classroom dictionary to find the meaning that fits with each picture. Complete the sentences.

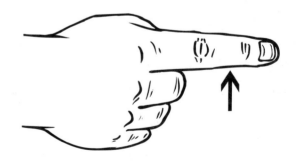

1. A digit is _____.

2. A digit is _____.

# Make Connections

Read the sentence below. Think about the meaning of each **bold** term. Then, check the Student Dictionary.

> In the **fraction** $\frac{3}{4}$, the **numerator** is 3, and the **denominator** is 4.

Underline the better ending to each sentence.

1. The numerator is the number
   A. above the line in a fraction.
   B. below the line in a fraction.

2. The denominator tells how many
   A. equal parts are in the whole.
   B. numerators are in the whole.

3. A fraction is
   A. part of a whole.
   B. a small number.

4. A numerator shows how many
   A. parts of the whole are counted.
   B. equal parts are in the whole.

5. The denominator is 2 in
   A. the fraction $\frac{2}{3}$.
   B. the fraction $\frac{1}{2}$.

Draw a picture of a cracker broken into two equal pieces. Write a fraction to name one of the pieces. Add the labels *numerator* and *denominator* to your fraction.

# Make Connections

Look at the pictures and captions. Think about the meaning of each **bold** term. Then, check the Student Dictionary.

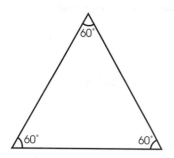

An **equilateral triangle** has sides of the same length and **angles** of the same size.

A **right triangle** has two perpendicular sides. They meet to form a 90 degree angle.

Circle the picture that answers the question.

1. Which picture shows a right triangle?

A.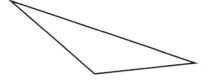

B.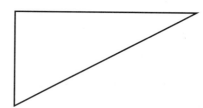

2. Which picture shows an angle?

A.

B.

3. Which picture shows an equilateral triangle.

A.

B.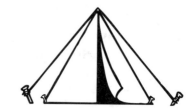

# Make Connections

Read the paragraph below. Think about the meaning of each **bold** word. Then, check the Student Dictionary.

> 5, 10, 15, 20, 25
>
> When you count by fives, you are saying **multiples** of 5. Each multiple is a **product** of 5 and another number. When you learn **multiplication** facts, you are learning lists of multiples.

Circle *Yes* or *No* for each question. Write your reason on the line.

1. When you multiply two numbers, do you get a product?   Yes   No

   _____

2. Is multiplication like subtraction?                   Yes   No

   _____

3. Is 12 a multiple of 2?                                 Yes   No

   _____

4. Is 12 a product of 6 and 6?                            Yes   No

   _____

5. Is a multiple of a number smaller than that number?    Yes   No

   _____

# Make Connections

Read the example and the sentence. Think about the meaning of each **bold** word. Then, check the Student Dictionary.

$$3\overline{)14}^{\,4\,R2}$$

In this **division** problem, the **quotient** is 4 with a **remainder** of 2.

Follow each instruction

1. Circle all of the examples that show division.

    15 ÷ 3          $\frac{2}{5}$          15 + 15          7 – 4          $4\overline{)20}$

2. Three friends want to share 7 grapes. Draw a picture to show the number of grapes each friend will get. Write a vocabulary word to label what is left over.

3. Look back at the example at the top of this page. Use words and numbers to explain why the quotient is 4 R2.

    _____

    _____

 **Challenge!**

Read the sentence below. Write or draw to show what it means.

The quotient in a division problem shows the number of equal parts.

Words Every Third Grader Needs to Know!

# Make Connections

Read the paragraph below. Think about the meaning of each **bold** term. Then, check the Student Dictionary.

Three or more line segments connect to form a shape called a **polygon**. One kind of polygon is a **rectangle**. A rectangle has 4 sides and 4 right angles. A **pentagon** is another kind of polygon. It has 5 sides. A **hexagon** has 6 sides. An **octagon** has 8 sides.

Label each polygon.

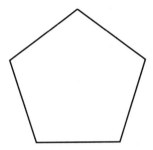

1. _____

2. _____

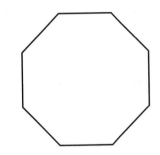

3. _____

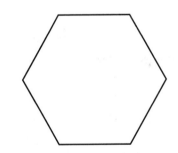

4. _____

Look at the shape below. Is it a polygon? Write *Yes* or *No*. Then, write your reason.

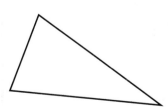

_____

_____

_____

# Make Connections

Read each pair of vocabulary words. Write the words where they fit in the sentences. Check the Student Dictionary for any meanings that you need.

**1.** division                multiplication

How many groups of 6 are in the whole group of 120? Use _____ to find out. How many are in the whole group if you have 20 groups of 6? Use _____ to find out.

**2.** rectangle                measurement

We made a _____ of the area of the rug. The rug is in the shape of a _____.

**3.** denominator                decimal point

The _____ of the fraction $\frac{3}{10}$ is 10. The fraction can also be written with a _____ followed by a 3.

**4.** right triangle                angle

This three-sided shape must be a _____ because one _____ is 90 degrees.

**5.** perimeter                equilateral triangle

To find the _____ of the _____, multiply the length of each side by 3.

Read the sentence you completed in question 5. Draw a picture to show what that sentence means.

# Play With Words

## Letter by Letter

Choose the word that fits with each clue. Write it letter by letter. Some letters will be inside circles.

| fraction | hexagon | product |
|----------|---------|---------|
| quotient | polygons | multiples |

1. $15 \div 3 = ?$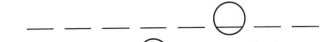

2.

3. A triangle and a rectangle

4. 3, 6, 9, 12, 15

5. $10 \times 5 = ?$

6. $\frac{12}{13}$

Write the circled letters in order on the blanks. You will find a word to complete the message.

You must be an __ __ __ __ __ __!

# Play With Words

## Code Words

Choose the word that fits in each sentence. Circle its letter.

1. The number 4 is a ___.
   - **f** digit
   - **g** fraction
   - **h** decimal point

2. A polygon with five sides is a ___.
   - **h** right triangle
   - **i** pentagon
   - **j** octagon

3. The letter **L** has ___ line segments.
   - **e** diagonal
   - **f** octagon
   - **g** perpendicular

4. The fraction $\frac{2}{3}$ has the ___ 2.
   - **s** denominator
   - **t** quotient
   - **u** numerator

5. A ___ cuts a rectangle into two right triangles.
   - **r** diagonal
   - **s** measurement
   - **t** perimeter

6. ___ is measured in square units.
   - **c** Perimeter
   - **d** Angle
   - **e** Area

Write the circled letters in order. You will find a word for a number or a shape. The word also tells what math students do.

_____

# Important Science and Health Words You Need to Know!

Use this list to keep track of how well you know the new words.

0 = Don't Know    1 = Know It Somewhat    2 = Know It Well

___ ___ adaptation
___ ___ asteroid
___ ___ axis
___ ___ carnivore
___ ___ comet
___ ___ condense
___ ___ decomposer
___ ___ ecosystem
___ ___ evaporate
___ ___ extinct
___ ___ food web
___ ___ gas
___ ___ habitat
___ ___ heat
___ ___ herbivore
___ ___ hibernate
___ ___ humidity
___ ___ liquid

___ ___ matter
___ ___ nutrient
___ ___ orbit
___ ___ perspire
___ ___ precipitation
___ ___ predator
___ ___ prey
___ ___ producer
___ ___ reproduce
___ ___ revolve
___ ___ rotate
___ ___ solar system
___ ___ solid
___ ___ species
___ ___ tilt
___ ___ water cycle
___ ___ water vapor

# Explore a Word

Name _____

Follow these steps.

1. Read the paragraph below. Think about the meaning of the **bold** word.

> Food contains fats, proteins, sugar, starch, vitamins, and minerals. These are the **nutrients** your body uses to grow and to stay healthy. Water is another nutrient that your body must have.

2. What do you think the word means? Write your idea.

   **nutrient:** _____

   _____

3. Write a sentence with the word **nutrient**. Show what it means.

   _____

   _____

4. Check the meaning of **nutrient** in the Student Dictionary.

5. If your sentence in step 3 matches the meaning, put a ✓ after it. If your sentence does not match the meaning, write a better sentence.

   _____

   _____

6. Make a simple drawing to show the meaning of **nutrient**.

# Explore a Word

Read the paragraph below. Think about the meaning of the **bold** word.
Then, check the Student Dictionary.

Plants and animals have many **adaptations** that help them
stay alive. For example, a cactus has roots that spread out to
collect water in the ground. Its roots are an **adaptation** that
allows the cactus to live in dry lands. Another example of an
adaptation is an eagle's sharp eyesight. This adaptation helps the
bird hunt small animals when it flies high above the ground.

Fill out this web to show your ideas about adaptations.

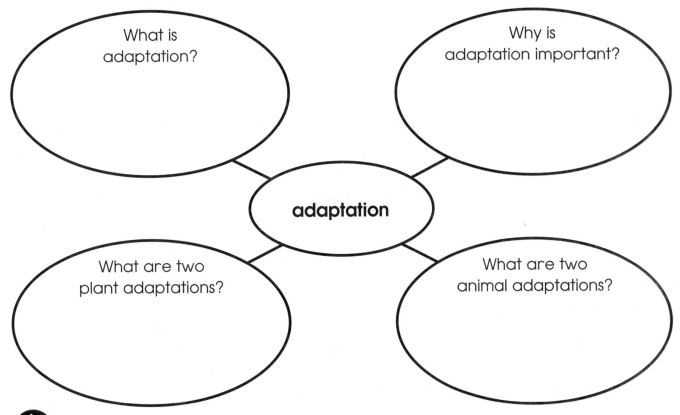

What is
adaptation?

Why is
adaptation important?

adaptation

What are two
plant adaptations?

What are two
animal adaptations?

## 🔍 Word Alert!

A suffix is a word part added to the end of a word. The suffix *-ation* is
added to the base word *adapt*. Complete the sentence with *adapt* and
*adaptation*.

Thick fur is one <sup>(1.)</sup> _____ that helps mammals to

<sup>(2.)</sup> _____ to cold weather.

# Explore a Word

Read the sentence below. Think about the meaning of the **bold** word. Then, check the Student Dictionary.

> Saber-toothed cats were large mammals that lived in many parts of the world. They became **extinct** about ten thousand years ago.

Answer each question.

1. What are two animals that are extinct?

   _____

2. What are two reasons that living things become extinct?

   _____

   _____

3. What is the difference between a dead plant and an extinct plant?

   _____

4. How do scientists decide that a living thing might become extinct?

   _____

   _____

## Word Alert!

A suffix is a word part added to the end of a word. The suffix *-ion* is added to the base word *extinct* to form the word *extinction*. Complete the sentences with *extinct* and *extinction*.

The <sup>(1.)</sup> _____ of living things has been happening for millions of years. Scientists do not always know why some life forms become <sup>(2.)</sup> _____ .

Words Every Third Grader Needs to Know!

# Compare Words

Read the sentences below. Think about the meaning of each **bold** term. Then, check the Student Dictionary.

> Some animals are **herbivores**. They eat fruits, seeds, grass, and plants. These animals are eaten by **carnivores**.

Circle the word that completes each sentence.

1. Lions and tigers are (herbivores/carnivores).

2. Cows and sheep are (herbivores/carnivores).

3. Owls are (herbivores/carnivores) that catch and eat mice.

4. Some kinds of (herbivores/carnivores) live in herds that roam over grasslands to graze.

5. Wolves are (herbivores/carnivores) that hunt in groups called *packs*.

## Challenge!

The word part *vore* is in *herbivore* and *carnivore*. What do you think this word part means? What do you think an *omnivore* is? Check your ideas in a classroom dictionary. Then, draw to show what you have learned about the words *herbivore*, *carnivore*, and *omnivore*.

# Compare Words

Read the paragraph below. Think about the meaning of each **bold** word. Then, check the Student Dictionary.

> Have you ever seen a pet cat crouch and move slowly before pouncing on a toy? In the wild, a cat is a **predator** that hides and moves slowly to sneak up on its **prey**.

Read each sentence. Copy each underlined word and label it *predator* or *prey*.

**1.** A <u>spider</u> spins a web to trap <u>insects</u>.

_____

**2.** <u>Deer</u> are fast enough to outrun <u>wolves</u>.

_____

**3.** Watch a <u>robin</u> pull an <u>earthworm</u> out of the ground.

_____

**4.** A <u>polar bear</u> hunts for <u>seals</u> under the ice.

_____

**5.** <u>Sharks</u> are food for some kinds of <u>seals</u>.

_____

*Words Every Third Grader Needs to Know!*

# Make Connections

Read the paragraphs below. Think about the meaning of each **bold** word. Then, check the Student Dictionary.

> Living things and nonliving things are connected in every **ecosystem**. For example, sunlight, soil, water, and air are nonliving things. They are used by plants to produce food. Plants are **producers**. Herbivores eat plants, and then carnivores eat herbivores.
>
> When plants and animals die, their remains are broken down into nutrients that return to the soil. The living things that break down the material are called **decomposers**. Most decomposers are too tiny to see.

Underline the better ending to each sentence.

1. An example of an ecosystem is
   A. a pond.
   B. a swimming pool.

2. An example of a producer is
   A. soil.
   B. a tree.

3. Producers use sunlight to
   A. make water warm.
   B. make food.

4. We can see the work of decomposers in
   A. rotting fruit.
   B. a plant bud.

5. Decomposers are needed to
   A. enrich the soil for producers.
   B. provide a source of food for carnivores.

# Make Connections

Read the paragraph below. Think about the meaning of each **bold** term. Then, check the Student Dictionary.

> The living things in a **habitat** must find food, stay safe, and **reproduce**. The **species** that share a habitat form **food webs**. Plants are the start of every food web. They produce food for all kinds of animals. Plant-eating animals, in turn, are eaten by other animals. Every habitat has food webs that show connections among the species.

Complete each sentence with a vocabulary word.

1. An oak tree produces acorns so that the tree will

   _____.

2. Fish in the deep ocean live in a dark, cold _____.

3. A caterpillar eats a leaf. A bird eats the caterpillar. The leaf, caterpillar, and bird form a chain that is part of a bigger

   _____.

4. The Northern flying squirrel and the Southern flying squirrel look alike. But they are two different _____.

5. A male and female insect must be of the same species in order to

   _____.

6. In the habitat of a freshwater lake, green plants, insects, fish, birds, reptiles, and mammals are all linked in a _____.

# Make Connections

Read the paragraph below. Think about the meaning of each **bold** word. Then, check the Student Dictionary.

> Air is **matter**. Water is matter. You and everything around you is made of matter. Matter is anything that takes up space and has weight. It can be in the form of a **solid**, a **liquid**, or a **gas**.

Read each question. Circle the answer.

1. What form of matter is inside a balloon?          solid    liquid    gas

2. What form of matter is orange juice?          solid    liquid    gas

3. What form of matter is rain?          solid    liquid    gas

4. What form of matter is an ice cube?          solid    liquid    gas

5. What form of matter spreads out to fill a room?          solid    liquid    gas

6. What form of matter keeps its shape?          solid    liquid    gas

 **Look It Up!**

We use one meaning of *matter* to talk about science. We use another meaning of *matter* in everyday language. Look up *matter* in a classroom dictionary. Write the meaning that fits with each phrase below. Use your own words to tell what the phrase means.

1. a matter to discuss: _____

2. a state of matter: _____

# Make Connections

Read the paragraphs below. Think about the meaning of each **bold** term. Then, check the Student Dictionary.

> Did you drink some water today? The water you drank was extremely old—as old as the Earth itself! Water moves from one place to another through a process called the **water cycle**.
>
> Water is a liquid in oceans, rivers, and other bodies of water. The sun's heat causes water to **evaporate** and change into a gas. The gas rises. As it is cooled, the gas **condenses** back into a liquid. It falls as rain or another form of **precipitation**.

Add labels to explain what is shown in this diagram. Use all of the vocabulary words in your labels.

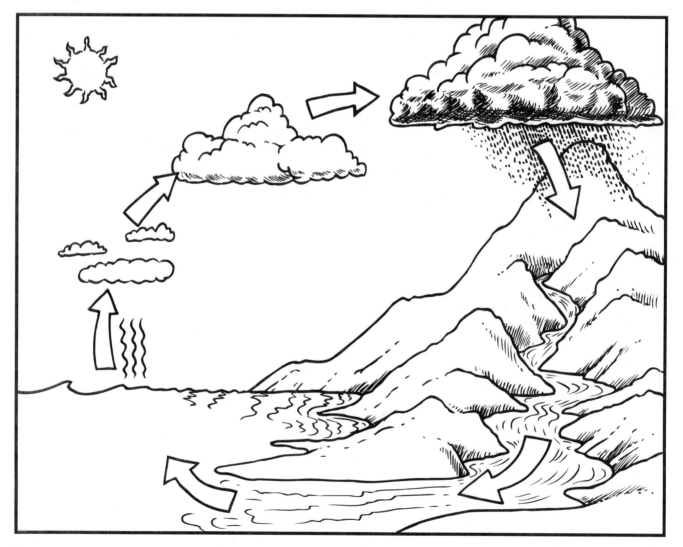

*Words Every Third Grader Needs to Know!*

# Make Connections

Read the paragraphs below. Think about the meaning of each **bold** term. Then, check the Student Dictionary.

> On a hot day, your body **perspires** through tiny holes in your skin. The liquid water on your skin changes into the gas called **water vapor**. The water vapor pulls heat away from your body and into the air. This is the body's way of cooling itself so that it does not become **overheated**. But liquid water doesn't evaporate if the air holds a lot of **humidity**. Then, your skin stays hot and sticky.
>
> Remember that when you perspire, you are losing water that your body needs. So be sure to drink plenty of water on hot days!

Complete each sentence with one or more words that make sense.

1. Water vapor is _____ in the form of a gas.

2. A body that cannot _____ could become overheated.

3. I can tell that I am perspiring when _____ on my skin.

4. On a day with high humidity, the air _____ water vapor.

5. To avoid overheating, a person should _____ and find shade.

# Make Connections

Look at the diagram. Think about the meaning of each **bold** word in the captions. Then, check the Student Dictionary.

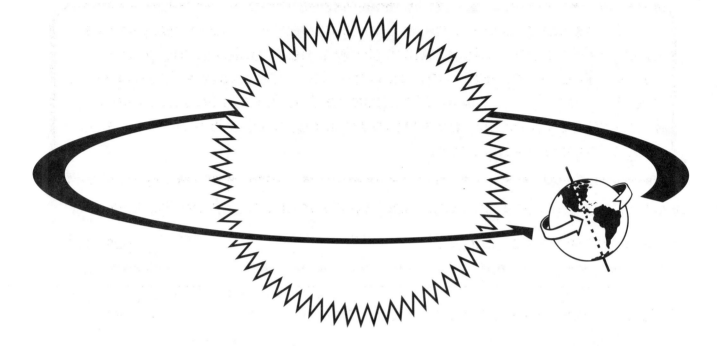

Earth **tilts**.
Earth **rotates**.
The **axis** is like a line through the North and South Poles.
Earth **revolves** around the Sun.
Its **orbit** is like a stretched circle.

Use the vocabulary words to complete the paragraph.

   It takes a year for the Earth to complete its (1.) _____

around the Sun. The planet is not straight, but (2.) _____

instead. This means that the Earth's northern half and southern half get

different amounts of sunlight during the year. As a result, there are

seasons. The Earth (3.) _____ around an imaginary line

called the (4.) _____. It completes a spin every 24 hours, or

a night and a day.

# Make Connections

Read the paragraph below. Think about the meaning of each **bold** term. Then, check the Student Dictionary.

> Our **solar system** has the Sun at its center. It also has planets and their moons. **Astronomers** study other bodies in the solar system, too. **Asteroids** are much smaller than planets. They are made of rock or metals. Most asteroids orbit the Sun between Mars and Jupiter. Icy **comets** make long, oval orbits from the far edges of the solar system.

Circle *Yes* or *No* for each question. Write your reason on the line.

**1.** Is a comet like a planet?                          Yes   No

_____

**2.** Is the solar system part of the Earth?            Yes   No

_____

**3.** Do all bodies in the solar system orbit the Sun?  Yes   No

_____

**4.** Are astronomers astronauts?                       Yes   No

_____

**5.** Is an asteroid a moon?                            Yes   No

_____

 **Look It Up!**

The vocabulary words *asteroid* and *astronomer* begin with the same letters. They come from Greek words having to do with stars. Look up the words below in a classroom dictionary. Circle the ones that have to do with stars or space.

| astound | astronaut | asthma | asterisk | astronomy |
| --- | --- | --- | --- | --- |

# Make Connections

Read each pair of vocabulary words. Write the words where they fit in the sentences. Check the Student Dictionary for any meanings that you need.

1. matter                decomposers

   The floor of a forest is covered with _____ at work on dead leaves and other _____.

2. water vapor        condense

   We cannot see the gas called _____. But we can see it _____ into drops of liquid water.

3. adaptation        extinct

   If a living thing cannot make an _____ to a new habitat, it might become _____.

4. orbit              solar system

   Planets and asteroids _____ the Sun at the center of the _____.

5. reproduce        nutrients

   All living things have ways to get _____ to turn into the energy they need to stay alive. They also have ways to _____ so that the species will continue.

Write a sentence with the vocabulary words *solid* and *liquid*. Then, write the sentence again leaving blanks for the words. Challenge a partner to complete your sentence.

_____

_____

# Play With Words

## Code Words

Choose the word that fits in each sentence. Circle its letter.

1. A plant eater is a ___.
   - **d** carnivore
   - **e** herbivore
   - **f** predator

2. The Earth ___ around the Sun.
   - **n** revolves
   - **o** tilts
   - **p** axis

3. Seashores and forests are ___.
   - **c** species
   - **d** nutrients
   - **e** ecosystems

4. Small mammals are often ___.
   - **r** prey
   - **s** producers
   - **t** extinct

5. Water vapor forms when liquid water ___.
   - **e** humidity
   - **f** condenses
   - **g** evaporates

6. ___ orbit the Sun.
   - **x** Astronomers
   - **y** Comets
   - **z** Solar systems

Write the circled letters in order. You will find a word to complete the sentence below.

Scientists study matter and _____.

# Play With Words

## Vocabulary Search

Use each clue to find a vocabulary word in the puzzle. The words go across and down. Then, write the words below.

Clues

1. Snow, rain, hail
2. All plants
3. A space scientist
4. Hawks, lions, sharks

5. Imaginary line through a planet
6. Communities of living things
7. Eaters and the eaten
8. Kinds of living things

| L | E | T | P | R | I | E | A | Z | N | P | T | O |
|---|---|---|---|---|---|---|---|---|---|---|---|---|
| F | G | O | O | R | P | C | U | F | E | R | S | S |
| A | M | A | S | T | R | O | N | O | M | E | R | W |
| E | B | I | X | C | O | S | Y | O | Z | C | T | I |
| A | X | I | S | P | D | Y | K | D | O | I | D | L |
| F | W | L | P | N | U | S | N | W | H | P | A | N |
| C | U | I | E | E | C | T | M | E | B | I | D | E |
| E | J | I | C | S | E | E | T | B | G | T | R | O |
| L | A | P | I | T | R | M | V | Q | U | A | J | T |
| O | T | Q | E | W | S | F | A | V | C | T | U | D |
| I | M | D | S | H | E | S | L | O | P | I | R | B |
| M | O | Y | V | P | R | E | D | A | T | O | R | S |
| A | P | E | H | I | K | A | N | U | S | N | I | E |

Answers

1. _____
2. _____
3. _____
4. _____

5. _____
6. _____
7. _____
8. _____

# Important Technology Words You Need to Know!

Use this list to keep track of how well you know the new words.

0 = Don't Know        1 = Know It Somewhat        2 = Know It Well

___ ___ brainstorm

___ ___ browser

___ ___ engineering

___ ___ force

___ ___ gear

___ ___ Internet

___ ___ invention

___ ___ model

___ ___ pulley

___ ___ recycle

___ ___ reduce

___ ___ reuse

___ ___ simple machine

___ ___ ramp

___ ___ wheel and axle

# Explore a Word

Follow these steps.

**1.** Read the paragraph below. Think about the meaning of the **bold** word.

> Push a toy car across the floor. Pull it back. You are making the car move by putting a **force** on it. Forces act on everything. Forces make things move and make them stop moving. The force called *gravity* is holding you on the Earth right now.

**2.** What do you think the word means? Write your idea.

**force:** _____

_____

**3.** Write a sentence with the word **force**. Show what it means.

_____

_____

**4.** Check the meaning of **force** in the Student Dictionary.

**5.** If your sentence in step 3 matches the meaning, put a ✓ after it. If your sentence does not match the meaning, write a better sentence.

_____

_____

**6.** Make a simple drawing to show the meaning of **force**.

# Explore a Word

Read the paragraphs below. Think about the meaning of the **bold** word. Then, check the Student Dictionary.

> Where can you find technology? Just look around you. Technology is anything that people have made to solve a problem. A pencil, an eraser, a carpet, and a computer are all technologies.
>
> How do people come up with technologies? First, they ask, "Can we make something to solve this problem?" Next, they **brainstorm** with others to come up with ideas for solving the problem.

Fill out the chart to show your understanding of the word *brainstorm*.

| 1. What is brainstorming? | 2. Why is *brainstorm* a good name? |
|---|---|
| 3. How is brainstorming different from thinking? | 4. What do people do after they brainstorm? |

# Explore a Word

Read the sentences below. Think about the meaning of the **bold** word. Then, check the Student Dictionary.

> Brady has a great idea for a hockey stick designed for beginning players. But first, he must build a **model** to see how well it works.

Complete each sentence with your own idea.

1. It is important to build a model before _____.

2. We tested the model of the machine to see _____.

3. A design is different from a model because _____

_____.

4. Models do not always _____.

 ## Look It Up!

The word *model* is used to talk about technology. It is also used to talk about other things. Look up *model* in a classroom dictionary. Write the meaning that fits with each phrase below. Use your own words to tell what the phrase means.

1. a model for a new machine: _____

2. a model of car: _____

3. a fashion model: _____

# Compare Words

Read the sentences below. Think about the meaning of each **bold** word. Then, check the Student Dictionary.

> **Inventors** use their knowledge of science to come up with ideas for new products. **Engineers** use science to figure out how to make new products.

Circle the word that completes each sentence.

1. A government grants a patent to any (inventor/engineer) of a new product. A patent is the sole right to make or sell a product.

2. Thomas Edison had more than 1,000 patents for products. He was the most famous (inventor/engineer) of his time.

3. Some (inventors/engineers) design bridges and tunnels.

4. The people who design video games are called software (inventors/engineers).

5. The Wright brothers were the (inventors/engineers) of the first motor-powered airplane. Before their first successful flight, they had been (inventors/engineers) who always worked with machines.

 **Challenge!**

You can see the base word *engine* in *engineer*. What does an engine have to do with the field of engineering? Use a dictionary to find the answer. Write it below.

_____

_____

# Make Connections

Read the sentence below. Think about the meaning of each **bold** word. Then, check the Student Dictionary.

> Use a **browser** to reach a Web site on the **Internet**.

Complete each sentence with your own idea.

1. My computer is connected to the Internet. That means I can _____

   _____.

2. I type an address in the field displayed by the browser. The browser quickly _____

   _____.

3. The browser takes charge of all links on a Web page. If I click on

   _____

   _____.

4. The Internet covers the world. That means that I might _____

   _____.

5. The browser on our school computers is called _____

   _____.

## Word Alert!

The prefix *inter-* means "between." Underline each word with *inter-* in the sentence below. Use your own words to tell what the sentence means. Do not use any of the underlined words in your sentence.

The Internet has many interactive games for interconnected users.

_____

_____

# Make Connections

Read the sentences below. Think about the meaning of each **bold** word. Then, check the Student Dictionary.

> Movers use a **ramp** to load heavy furniture into a truck. Like other **simple machines**, a ramp makes work easier.

Circle *Yes* or *No* for each question. Write your reason on the line.

1. Do all simple machines have moving parts?               Yes   No

   _____

2. Is a car an example of a simple machine?                Yes   No

   _____

3. Does an object on a ramp move a shorter distance
   than an object that is lifted straight up?              Yes   No

   _____

4. Is a ladder an example of a ramp?                       Yes   No

   _____

5. Must you use force to move an object up a ramp?         Yes   No

   _____

Draw a picture of a ramp. Write a caption to tell how it is used.

# Make Connections

Look at each picture and the captions. Think about the meaning of each **bold** term. Then, check the Student Dictionary.

| Three simple machines make work easier. |
| --- |

**wheel and axle**

**pulley**

**gear**

Use the vocabulary words to complete the paragraph.

Some kinds of simple machines are made with wheels. A rod is inserted into the center of a wheel in a (1.) _____. One turn of the axle causes the wheel to move a greater distance than the axle moves. Pulling down on the rope of a (2.) _____ lifts a weight on the other end. Turning one wheel of a (3.) _____ causes the other wheel to turn.

Each item below works because of a simple machine. Write the vocabulary word that names the simple machine.

1. window blinds: _____

2. bicycle chain: _____

3. roller skate: _____

# Make Connections

Read the poster below. Think about the meaning of each **bold** word. Then, check the Student Dictionary.

We need a healthy environment. We need to manage our waste.

We all can help if we practice the 3 R's!

**Reduce.** Avoid wasteful packaging. Buy and use less stuff.

**Reuse.** Find new uses for things. Buy used items. They can be as good as new ones.

**Recycle.** Don't throw away anything that can be made into something new.

Answer each question.

1. What are three things you try to recycle?

   _____

2. How can you reduce your use of paper and plastic cups?

   _____

3. What are two ways that outgrown clothing can be reused?

   _____

   _____

## Word Alert!

The prefix *re-* means "again" in each word below. Use the word *again* as you write a meaning for each word.

1. reuse: _____

2. renew: _____

3. refill: _____

# Make Connections

Read each pair of vocabulary words. Write the words where they fit in the sentences. Check the Student Dictionary for any meanings that you need.

**1.** gears        engineers

The earliest _____ were made of wood. But

_____ improved the simple machines with new

materials.

**2.** brainstorm        reduce

The students will _____ ways to _____ the

amount of paper they use.

**3.** model        inventor

The _____ drew a design for a silent skateboard. Next,

she made a _____ to see if the skateboard worked.

**4.** simple machines        pulleys

Ramps, wheels and axles, gears, and _____ are kinds of

_____.

**5.** Internet        browser

A _____ is software installed on a computer. It helps

that computer send and receive information from the

_____.

Look at the list on page 35. Choose two vocabulary words that are not on this page. Write a sentence with those two words.

_____

_____

# Play With Words

## Code Words

Choose the word that fits in each sentence. Circle its letter.

1. Computers connected worldwide form the ___.
   - c inventor
   - d Internet
   - e browser

2. A ___ raises a flag on a flagpole.
   - d ramp
   - e pulley
   - f gear

3. A tug on a rope is ___.
   - s a force
   - t a pulley
   - u simple machine

4. A wheelchair ramp is a ___.
   - i simple machine
   - j gear
   - k recycle

5. ___ build models to test.
   - e Browsers
   - f Forces
   - g Engineers

6. Can you ___ your use of paper?
   - l reuse
   - m brainstorm
   - n reduce

Write the circled letters in order. You will find the word that answers this question: *What do you call the plan for a new technology?*

a _____

# Play With Words

## Letter by Letter

Choose the word that fits with each clue. Write it letter by letter. Some letters will be inside circles.

| engineer | wheel | inventor |
|---|---|---|
| force | recycle | pulley |

1. Do this with glass and plastic.   — — — Ⓞ — — —

2. This is a push or a pull.   — Ⓞ — — —

3. This helps you lift something.   — Ⓞ — — — —

4. This is attached to an axle.   — Ⓞ — — —

5. This worker designs software.   — — — Ⓞ — — — —

6. This worker has a new idea.   — Ⓞ — — — — — —

Write the circled letters in order on the blanks. You will find a message.

— — —    — — —!

# Important Language Arts Words You Need to Know!

Use this list to keep track of how well you know the new words.

0 = Don't Know        1 = Know It Somewhat        2 = Know It Well

___ ___ adjective

___ ___ antonym

___ ___ biography

___ ___ context clue

___ ___ definition

___ ___ dialogue

___ ___ draft

___ ___ fact

___ ___ fantasy

___ ___ fiction

___ ___ haiku

___ ___ homophone

___ ___ index

___ ___ inference

___ ___ journal

___ ___ nonfiction

___ ___ noun

___ ___ opinion

___ ___ plural

___ ___ pourquoi tale

___ ___ prefix

___ ___ proofread

___ ___ publish

___ ___ quotation marks

___ ___ revise

___ ___ sequence

___ ___ singular

___ ___ suffix

___ ___ synonym

___ ___ verb

# Explore a Word

Follow these steps.

1. Read the paragraph below. Think about the meaning of the **bold** word.

> When I read stories, I like to think about things that the author is hinting at. I might ask, "Why doesn't that character share her toys?" Or, "Should that character be trusted?" Stories seem more interesting when I try to make **inferences** about the characters.

2. What do you think the word means? Write your idea.

    **inference:** _____

    _____

3. Write a sentence with the word **inference**. Show what it means.

    _____

    _____

4. Check the meaning of **inference** in the Student Dictionary.

5. If your sentence in step 3 matches the meaning, put a ✓ after it. If your sentence does not match the meaning, write a better sentence.

    _____

    _____

6. Make a simple drawing to show the meaning of **inference**.

# Explore a Word

Read the paragraph below. Think about the meaning of the **bold** word.
Then, check the Student Dictionary.

Would you describe today as hot, cold, windy, sunny, boring,
exciting, wonderful, or horrible? Words that describe a person, a
place, or a thing are called **adjectives**.

Complete the web to show your understanding of the word *adjective*.

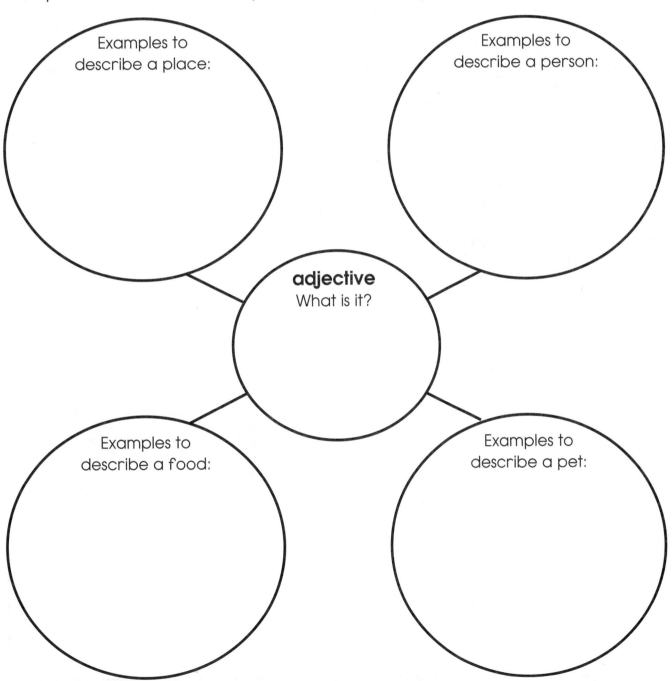

Examples to describe a place:

Examples to describe a person:

**adjective**
What is it?

Examples to describe a food:

Examples to describe a pet:

# Explore a Word

Read the poem and the caption. Think about the meaning of the **bold** word. Then, check the Student Dictionary.

> Listen to the brook
> as it whispers and giggles,
> sharing its secrets.
>
> A **haiku** is a three-line poem. Often, it describes a simple scene in nature. Each line in the poem has a certain number of syllables. There are 5 syllables in the first line, 7 syllables in the second line, and 5 syllables in the third line.

Follow each instruction.

1. Use your own words to tell what the haiku above is about.

_____

2. Read the lines below. Underline the one that could be in a haiku.

   A. on a snow-covered tree branch
   B. dogs barking, yipping, leaping, and spinning

3. Write the first line of a haiku about rain.

_____

4. List three topics you might write about in a haiku.

_____

5. Draw a picture of something to describe in a haiku. Then, write the haiku.

Words Every Third Grader Needs to Know!

# Compare Words

Read the chart. Think about the meaning of each **bold** word. Then, check the Student Dictionary.

| **Prefix** | Meaning | Examples | **Suffix** | Meaning | Examples |
|---|---|---|---|---|---|
| re- | "again" | redo, replay, refill | –er | "someone who does something" | worker, dancer, writer |
| un- | "not," "the opposite of" | undo, unfair, unbutton | –ly | "in a way that is" | slowly, softly, happily |

Follow each instruction.

1. Add the prefix *un-* to the base word *wise*. Write the word and its meaning.

   _____

2. Add the suffix *–er* to the base word *teach*. Write the word and its meaning.

   _____

3. Write the meaning of *reuse*. Write the prefix and base word in *reuse*.

   _____

4. Write the meaning of *quietly*. Write the base word and suffix in *quietly*.

   _____

5. Write the three parts in *unfairly*. Label the prefix and suffix.

   _____

6. Explain the difference between a prefix and a suffix.

   _____

# Compare Words

Read the sentences below. Think about the meaning of each **bold** word. Then, check the Student Dictionary.

*Easy* and *simple* are **synonyms**. *Easy* and *hard* are **antonyms**.

Read the sentence. Are the underlined words synonyms or antonyms? Circle the answer.

1. I like <u>hot</u> food, but this rice is too <u>spicy</u>!          synonyms   antonyms

2. The <u>cool</u> air is turning <u>warm</u>.          synonyms   antonyms

3. Should we talk <u>loudly</u> or <u>softly</u>?          synonyms   antonyms

4. Darla <u>smiled</u>, and her friends <u>grinned</u>.          synonyms   antonyms

5. That <u>big</u> house has <u>large</u> windows.          synonyms   antonyms

6. Is the dog's fur <u>short</u> or <u>long</u>?          synonyms   antonyms

7. Turn <u>left</u> first, and then <u>right</u>.          synonyms   antonyms

8. The <u>clever</u> fox has a <u>smart</u> plan.          synonyms   antonyms

 **Look It Up!**

Prefixes and suffixes are listed in a dictionary. Look up the prefix *anti-* (or *ant-*) in a classroom dictionary. How does its meaning help you remember the meaning of *antonym*?

_____

# Compare Words

Read the chart. Think about the meaning of each **bold** word. Then, check the Student Dictionary.

| A **noun** is a naming word. It names a person, place, or thing. | A **verb** shows what someone or something does or is. |
|---|---|
| Examples: person, boy, girl, children, doctor, place, city, street, mountain, thing, toy, book, fingernail, shoes | Examples: run, sit, dance, jump, talk, help, ask, read, wiggle, spin, play, write, be, is, are |

Read each sentence. Copy each underlined word. Then, write *noun* or *verb* after it.

1. We <u>watched</u> the exciting <u>game</u>.

   _____

2. Six <u>dancers</u> <u>twirled</u> fast!

   _____

3. <u>Cats</u> <u>stretch</u> and <u>yawn</u>.

   _____

4. My <u>mother</u> <u>is</u> a <u>teacher</u>.

   _____

5. The big yellow <u>house</u> <u>sits</u> on a <u>hill</u>.

   _____

 **Challenge!**

Explain to a partner the meaning of the sentence below.

The word *verb* is a noun.

# Compare Words

Read the chart. Think about the meaning of each **bold** word. Then, check the Student Dictionary.

| A **singular** noun names one person, place, or thing. | A **plural** noun names more than one person, place, or thing. |
| --- | --- |
| Examples: person, child, girl, boy, place, city, beach, library, thing, toy, daisy, foot, mouse | Examples: people, children, girls, boys, places, cities, beaches, libraries, things, toys, daisies, feet, mice |

Read each noun. Write *S* if it is singular. Write *P* if it is plural.

1. women ___
2. dogs ___
3. pennies ___
4. glass ___
5. chair ___

6. house ___
7. rabbit ___
8. bushes ___
9. dresses ___
10. wolves ___

 **Challenge!**

Look at each of the ten numbered nouns. If the noun is singular, write the plural form. If it is plural, write the singular form.

_____

_____

# Compare Words

Read the chart. Think about the meaning of each **bold** word. Then, check the Student Dictionary.

| Facts | Opinions |
|---|---|
| Pennsylvania is a state. <br> Winter begins in December. <br> Dogs are mammals. | Pennsylvania is beautiful! <br> I don't like winter sports. <br> Dogs are the best pets. |

Write *facts* or *opinions* to complete the sentences.

Statements that can be proved true are [1.] _____. You

can check [2.] _____ by looking in books. You cannot check

[3.] _____. They are what people think or feel. You can

agree or disagree with [4.] _____, but not with

[5.] _____.

Think of a sport or an animal. Write a fact about it. Then, write an opinion.

**1.** Fact: _____

**2.** Opinion: _____

# Make Connections

Read the paragraph below. Think about the meaning of each **bold** term. Then, check the Student Dictionary.

> When you read the **dialogue** in a story, how can you tell which character is speaking? Look for the words before and after the **quotation marks**. The words inside of the quotation marks are spoken by a character.

Read the dialogue below. Then, answer the questions.

> "Tonight, we're eating a special treat," announced Mama Mouse.
> "Pizza!" cried Andy Mouse.
> Allie Mouse said, "No, it must be strawberry cupcakes."
> "I'm afraid you're both mistaken," said Mama Mouse. "But you'll soon

**1.** Who is speaking the dialogue?

_____

**2.** What does Andy Mouse say, and how does he sound?

_____

**3.** Who says the words *Just follow me?* How can you tell?

_____

Write dialogue for the next part of the story. Give each character something to say. Use quotation marks correctly.

> Mama Mouse led the two children along the wall to the dark kitchen.
>
> _____
>
> _____
>
> _____

Words Every Third Grader Needs to Know!

# Make Connections

Read the paragraph below. Think about the meaning of each **bold** term.
Then, check the Student Dictionary.

> When you are reading and come to a word you don't know,
> what should you do? Try looking for a **context clue** before and
> after the word. You might even find a **definition** of the word. If
> you can't find context clues, then use a dictionary to look up the
> definition.

Read each sentence. Write a short meaning for the underlined word.
Circle the choice that tells whether you found a definition or a different
kind of context clue.

1. The teacher frowns at <u>unruly</u> behavior.

   _____   context clue   definition

2. Dress very warmly on <u>frigid</u> days.

   _____   context clue   definition

3. Some <u>botanists</u>, or plant scientists, study corn.

   _____   context clue   definition

4. <u>Clippers</u> were the fastest sailing ships of their time.

   _____   context clue   definition

5. "Ugh!" said Celia, making a face. "I <u>detest</u> worms."

   _____   context clue   definition

## Word Alert!

The three words below are in the same word family. They have related
meanings. Try to use at least two of the words in a sentence.

| definition | define | definite |
|---|---|---|

_____

_____

# Make Connections

Read the paragraph below. Think about the meaning of each **bold** word. Then, check the Student Dictionary.

> The chapters of **fiction** books and **nonfiction** books are listed in the table of contents at the front. Some nonfiction books have an **index** at the back. The listings in an index help readers find the pages that have particular facts.

Circle *Yes* or *No* for each question. Write your reason on the line.

**1.** Is fiction made up by an author?                                        Yes  No

_____

**2.** Are the listings in an index arranged by chapter?              Yes  No

_____

**3.** Could a book about butterflies be nonfiction?                   Yes  No

_____

**4.** Is nonfiction usually not true?                                          Yes  No

_____

**5.** Would a picture book about a talking rat have an index?     Yes  No

_____

 ## Word Alert!

The prefix *non-* means "not." How does knowing that help you remember the meaning of *nonfiction*?

_____

# Make Connections

Look at the pictures and captions. Think about the meaning of each **bold** term. Then, check the Student Dictionary.

**biography**

**pourquoi tale**

**fantasy**

**journal**

Underline the better ending to each sentence.

1. A biography is
   A. a fiction story about someone.
   B. a nonfiction story about someone.

2. You know you are reading a fantasy when
   A.  impossible things happen.
   B. characters speak dialogue.

3. The author of a journal writes
   A. articles for magazines and newspapers.
   B. facts and opinions about experiences.

4. The French word *pourquoi* means "why." The stories called *pourquoi tales* tell why
   A. something in nature came to be.
   B. animal characters act like people.

5. You could read a biography about
   A. a music star.
   B. dinosaurs.

# Make Connections

Read the tips below. Think about the meaning of each bold word. Then, check the Student Dictionary.

---

### Tips for Getting Your Story Ready to **Publish**

- Use a list or other plan to write your **draft**.

- As you **revise** your draft, pay attention to **sequence**. Make sure you are using helpful words like *first*, *next*, and *later that day*.

- As you **proofread**, look for **homophones**. It's easy to confuse *their*, *there*, and *they're*. Make sure you've spelled the word you mean.

---

Complete each sentence with a vocabulary word from above.

1. Look for correct use of capital letters when you _____.

2. A first try at putting ideas into writing is called a _____.

3. The time order in which things happen is the _____ of events.

4. When you _____ your writing, you share a final version with readers.

5. When you _____ your story, you make it better.

6. The words *right*, *write*, *rite*, and *wright* are _____.

 **Look It Up!**

The word *draft* has more than one meaning. Use a classroom dictionary to find three definitions. On another sheet of paper, draw three pictures to show three definitions of *draft*.

---

Words Every Third Grader Needs to Know!

# Play With Words

## Code Words

Choose the word that fits in each sentence. Circle its letter.

1. Use ___ to figure out word meanings.
   r   context clues
   s   haiku
   t   verbs

2. A word meaning is a ___.
   e   definition
   f   journal
   g   plural

3. The words *school* and *student* are ___.
   u   verbs
   v   nouns
   w   homophones

4. The word *replay* has a ___.
   g   nonfiction
   h   suffix
   i   prefix

5. A noun that names one thing is ___.
   s   singular
   t   synonym
   u   plural

6. A ___ is a kind of fiction.
   c   fact
   d   homophone
   e   fantasy

Write the circled letters in order. You will find the answer to this question: *What is good advice for any writer?*

_____!

# Play With Words

## Hidden Message

Read the clue. Find and circle the vocabulary word that matches the clue.

1. *read* and *reed*                           h o h o m o p h o n e s w i s

2. first, next, after that, last               t h e l e s e q u e n c e t t

3. *icy* and *frozen*                          e r k l i s y n o n y m s k e f

4. the *-ly* in *gladly*                       l o u r y o s u f f i x u c a

5. more than one                              n t m a k e c a p l u r a l k e w

6. antonym for *fact*                         i t h o o p i n i o n u t i t

Look back to find the letters you did NOT circle. Write them in order on the lines below to find a riddle and its answer.

___ ___ ___     ___ ___     ___ ___ ___     ___ ___ ___ ___ ___

___     ___ ___ ___     ___ ___ ___ ___ ___?

___ ___ ___ ___     ___ ___ ___'___     ___ ___ ___ ___

___ ___ ___ ___     ___ ___ ___ ___ ___ ___ ___     ___ ___!

# Important History Words You Need to Know!

Use this list to keep track of how well you know the new words.

0 = Don't Know          1 = Know It Somewhat          2 = Know It Well

__ __ ancient

__ __ archaeology

__ __ architecture

__ __ century

__ __ civilization

__ __ colonist

__ __ culture

__ __ custom

__ __ decade

__ __ explorer

__ __ festival

__ __ folktale

__ __ historian

__ __ human rights

__ __ Independence Day

__ __ Memorial Day

__ __ monument

__ __ myth

__ __ native

__ __ settlement

# Explore a Word

Follow these steps.

1. Read the sentences below. Think about the meaning of the **bold** term.

> People want their leaders to treat them fairly. Fair treatment is a basic **human right**.

2. What do you think the word means? Write your idea.

   **human rights:** _____

   _____

3. Write a sentence with the word **human rights**. Show what it means.

   _____

   _____

4. Check the meaning of **human rights** in the Student Dictionary.

5. If your sentence in step 3 matches the meaning, put a ✓ after it. If your sentence does not match the meaning, write a better sentence.

   _____

   _____

6. Make a simple drawing to show the meaning of **human rights**.

Words Every Third Grader Needs to Know!

# Explore a Word

Read the sentence below. Think about the meaning of the **bold** word.
Then, check the Student Dictionary.

> A **historian** wrote a book about everyday life long ago in our
> town.

Fill out this web to show your ideas about historians.

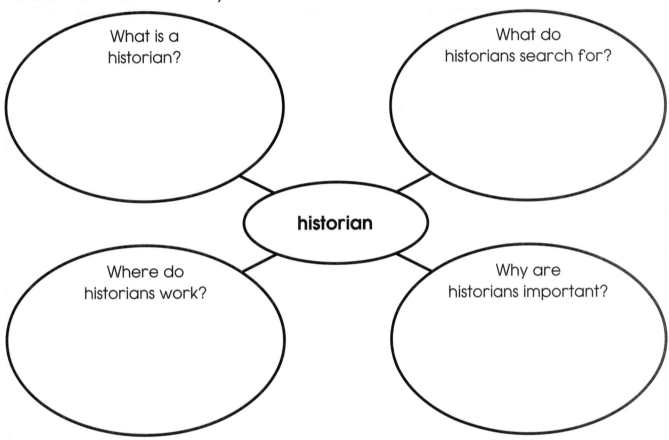

What is a
historian?

What do
historians search for?

historian

Where do
historians work?

Why are
historians important?

## 🔍 Word Alert!

A suffix is a word part added to the end of a word. The suffix *-ian* is
added to base words to name workers. Read each word below. Use the
base word to write what that worker does.

| historian | librarian | musician |
|-----------|-----------|----------|

_____

_____

_____

# Explore a Word

Read the paragraph below. Think about the meaning of the **bold** word. Then, check the Student Dictionary.

> People have always built **monuments** to heroes, events, and ideas. For example, the Washington Monument in Washington, D.C., honors George Washington. The Statue of Liberty in New York harbor is a symbol of welcome.

Think of a person from the past or a past event that deserves a monument. Design the monument. Then, complete the sentences to tell about it.

1. This monument is called _____.

2. It is made of _____.

3. The monument honors _____.

4. When people visit this monument, they will _____

_____.

# Compare Words

Read the sentence below. Think about the meaning of each **bold** word. Then, check the Student Dictionary.

> The first **decade** of the twentieth **century** lasted from 1900 to 1909.

Circle the word that completes each sentence.

1. A (century/decade) lasts 100 years.

2. We live in the twenty-first (century/decade).

3. A ten year old has lived for a (century/decade).

4. A world war took place during the (century/decade) of the 1940s.

5. Maura's great grandfather has lived for a (century/decade).

 **Look It Up!**

Use a classroom dictionary to find words that begin with *cent*. List three words that have to do with 100 parts or things. Tell a partner what each one has to do with the meaning "100."

_____

_____

_____

# Compare Words

Read the sentences below. Think about the meaning of each **bold** term. Then, check the Student Dictionary.

> Every year, on the last Monday in May, Americans observe **Memorial Day**. Every year on July 4, Americans celebrate **Independence Day**.

Read each sentence. Does it tell about Memorial Day or Independence Day? Circle the answer.

1. In 1776, a group of men met in Philadelphia. They signed a document declaring that they wanted to be free of Great Britain.

   Memorial Day          Independence Day

2. Americans gather to remember people in the armed forces who gave their lives for their country.

   Memorial Day          Independence Day

3. A day was set aside to honor the soldiers who had died in the Civil War (1861–1865).

   Memorial Day          Independence Day

4. Crowds cheer and clap as fireworks explode in the night sky.

   Memorial Day          Independence Day

5. Flowers and flags are placed on graves.

   Memorial Day          Independence Day

 **Word Alert!**

*Memorial* begins with *mem*, a root that has to do with thinking back on the past. Other words with that root are *memory* and *remember*. Read the sentence below. Underline the word with the root *mem*. Tell what you think it means.

A holiday is a way to commemorate an event from long ago.

# Make Connections

Read the paragraph below. Think about the meaning of each **bold** word. Then, check the Student Dictionary.

> **Explorers** from Europe first arrived in North and South America in the late 1400s. They found **native** people living in small **settlements** and in large cities. In the 1500s, European **colonists** began arriving to start their own settlements.

Complete each sentence with a vocabulary word from the paragraph above.

1. The country where you were born is your _____ land.

2. Christopher Columbus and Francisco Pizarro were _____ who claimed land for Spain.

3. The earliest _____ from England lived in Virginia and Massachusetts.

4. The Dutch built a _____ on land that is now New York City.

5. _____ made the first maps of rivers and lakes in North America.

## Word Alert!

Suffixes are word parts added to the end of a word. The suffixes *-ist* and *-er* can name people. Complete each sentence below with a word related to the underlined word.

1. People who live in a <u>colony</u> are called _____.

2. People who <u>explore</u> are called _____.

3. People who _____ are called <u>settlers</u>.

# Make Connections

Read the paragraph below. Think about the meaning of each **bold** word. Then, check the Student Dictionary.

> Do you like to eat Chinese food? What about Italian food? China and Italy have given the world different foods. Ways of cooking and eating are part of a people's **culture**. Other parts of a culture are **customs**, such as religious practices and **festivals**. A culture also includes stories, such as **folktales** and **myths**.

Circle *Yes* or *No* for each question. Write your reason on the line.

**1.** Is a festival usually a quiet time of prayer?         Yes   No

_____

**2.** Is storytelling part of a group's culture?         Yes   No

_____

**3.** Is a myth like a true adventure story?         Yes   No

_____

**4.** Does a folktale come from the "folk" of the past?         Yes   No

_____

**5.** Do people today have customs?         Yes   No

_____

*Words Every Third Grader Needs to Know!*

# Make Connections

Read the sentence below. Think about the meaning of each **bold** word. Then, check the Student Dictionary.

> Because of **archaeology**, we now know about the art, **architecture**, beliefs, and rulers of the **civilization** of the **ancient** Maya in Mexico and Central America.

Underline the better ending to each sentence.

1. If you studied archaeology, you would learn
   A. how to build skyscrapers.
   B. how to dig up objects buried long ago.

2. An ancient culture is
   A. very old.
   B. religious.

3. Signs of an ancient civilization are
   A. paintings in caves.
   B. half-buried buildings of a city.

4. You can see examples of architecture
   A. in the buildings around you.
   B. in styles of clothing.

5. Words that could describe any civilization are
   A. *ancient* and *important*.
   B. *large* and *organized*.

 **Challenge!**

Reread the sentence at the top of the page. Write two or three sentences to explain what the sentence means. Don't use any of the vocabulary words in your explanation.

_____

_____

_____

# Make Connections

Read each pair of vocabulary words. Write the words where they fit in the sentences. Check the Student Dictionary for any meanings that you need.

1. historian          century

   The _____ used photographs to show how the city has

   changed over the past _____.

2. monument          myth

   This statue is a _____ to the hero Jason of ancient

   _____.

3. archaeology          native

   How did the _____ people of Europe live thousands of

   years ago? Answers to that question come from

   _____.

4. civilization          architecture

   The _____ of ancient Greece produced

   _____ that is still copied today.

5. festival          culture

   With colorful costumes and marching bands, the people held a

   _____ to celebrate their native _____.

Write your own sentence with the two vocabulary words *colonist* and *settlement*. Then, write the sentence again with blanks instead of the words. Challenge a partner to complete your sentence.

_____

_____

# Play With Words

## Letter by Letter

Choose the word that fits with each clue. Write it letter by letter. Some letters will be inside circles.

| folktale | explorer | colonist | rights |
|----------|----------|----------|--------|
| ancient | decade | customs | |

1. Opposite of modern
   ⊖ _ _ _ _ _ _

2. Weddings, festivals, manners
   _ _ ⊖ _ _ _ _

3. Synonym for searcher
   _ _ ⊖ _ _ _ _ _

4. An old story
   _ ⊖ _ _ _ _ _ _

5. A settler from another land
   _ _ _ _ ⊖ _ _ _

6. Human ___
   _ _ ⊖ _ _ _

7. Ten years
   _ ⊖ _ _ _ _

Write the circled letters in order on the blanks. You will find the answer to this riddle: *What is full of holes yet still holds water?*

___    ___ ___ ___ ___ ___!

# Play With Words

## Code Words

Choose the word that fits in each sentence. Circle its letter.

1. The Fourth of July is also called
   ___.
   g  a monument
   h  Independence Day
   i  Memorial Day

2. The ___ had a few houses.
   a  settlement
   b  festival
   c  archaeology

3. Remember American soldiers
   on ___.
   p  Memorial Day
   q  historians
   r  architecture

4. Freedom of speech and
   religion are ___.
   n  native customs
   o  ancient cultures
   p  human rights

5. A museum of ___ shows
   ancient objects.
   c  monuments
   d  architecture
   e  archaeology

6. The ___ of ancient Rome lasted
   for centuries.
   m  archaeology
   n  civilization
   o  decades

Write the circled letters in order on the line. You will complete a question that a historian asks.

*What really did _____?*

# Important Geography Words You Need to Know!

Use this list to keep track of how well you know the new words.

0 = Don't Know          I = Know It Somewhat          2 = Know It Well

___ ___ capital
___ ___ cliff
___ ___ climate
___ ___ coastal
___ ___ continent
___ ___ county
___ ___ crop
___ ___ desert
___ ___ elevation
___ ___ environment
___ ___ grassland
___ ___ harbor
___ ___ kilometer
___ ___ landform
___ ___ local
___ ___ mountain pass
___ ___ mesa
___ ___ natural resource

___ ___ North America
___ ___ plain
___ ___ port
___ ___ scale
___ ___ tide
___ ___ valley
___ ___ weather

# Explore a Word

Follow these steps.

1. Read the sentence below. Think about the meaning of the **bold** word.

> People and other living things need an **environment** with clean water.

2. What do you think the word means? Write your idea.

**environment:** _____

_____

3. Write a sentence with the word **environment**. Show what it means.

_____

_____

4. Check the meaning of **environment** in the Student Dictionary.

5. If your sentence in step 3 matches the meaning, put a ✓ after it. If your sentence does not match the meaning, write a better sentence.

_____

_____

6. Make a simple drawing to show the meaning of **environment**.

# Compare Words

Read the sentence below. Think about the meaning of each **bold** word. Then, check the Student Dictionary.

> Our **climate** has cold **weather** for several months each year.

Read the sentence. Does it tell about climate or weather? Circle the answer.

1. Dark clouds mean it is going to rain.       climate    weather

2. Rain falls almost every day of the year.       climate    weather

3. All year, days are hot, and nights are cool.     climate    weather

4. There is a wet season and a dry season.       climate    weather

5. The sky is sunny and bright today.       climate    weather

6. Plants grow all year.       climate    weather

7. Strong winds blew down trees.       climate    weather

8. A big snowstorm buried roads.       climate    weather

Answer the question below with your own idea.

What is the weather like in the climate where you live?

_____

_____

# Compare Words

Look at the pictures and captions. Think about the meaning of each **bold** word. Then, check the Student Dictionary.

desert

grassland

Circle the word that completes each sentence.

1. Some (deserts, grasslands) are in climates that have a rainy season.

2. The plants of a (desert, grassland) can live without much water.

3. Some (deserts, grasslands) have huge hills of sand.

4. Many natural (deserts, grasslands) have been turned into farms.

5. A (desert, grassland) may be hot or cold, but it is always dry.

6. Many animals live underground in a hot (desert, grassland) because there is little shade to keep them cool.

##  Word Alert!

Two words put together are called a *compound word*. One of the vocabulary words is a compound word. Write a meaning for it. Include both of the smaller words in your meaning.

_____

# Make Connections

Look at the picture and caption. Think about the meaning of each **bold** word. Then, check the Student Dictionary.

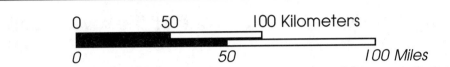

The **scale** on a map shows distances in miles and **kilometers**.

Underline the better ending to each sentence.

1. Mapmakers use a scale to show
   A. that miles and kilometers are both measures of distance.
   B. how real-life distances compare to lengths on the map.

2. A distance of 50 kilometers might be shown on a map as
   A. 2 inches.
   B. 30 miles.

3. An example of a scale is
   A. 1 inch equals 10 miles.
   B. 1 kilometer equals 1,000 meters.

4. Use a scale to measure the distance
   A. in kilometer-miles.
   B. in miles or in kilometers.

5. A kilometer is
   A. shorter than a mile.
   B. longer than a mile.

 **Look It Up!**

Look up the word *scale* in a classroom dictionary. You will find separately numbered entries. Use three of the definitions to complete the sentences below.

1. Use a balance scale to _____.

2. Use a scale of distance to _____.

3. The scales on a fish _____.

Name _____

# Make Connections

Read the sentence below. Think about the meaning of each **bold** term. Then, check the Student Dictionary.

> The **continent** of **North America** is one of the seven continents on the Earth.

Read the place names. List each one under the correct heading.

| | | |
|---|---|---|
| Canada | Europe | Australia |
| Asia | Antarctica | Central America |
| Greenland | Mexico | South America |
| North America | Caribbean Islands | Africa |
| United States | | |

| Continents | North America |
|---|---|
| | |

# Make Connections

Read the sentence below. Think about the meaning of each **bold** term. Then, check the Student Dictionary.

> Soil is a **natural resource** that farmers need to grow **crops**.

Complete each sentence with one or more words that make sense.

1. Wood is a natural resource because it comes

   _____ .

2. People use natural resources to

   _____ things.

3. Crops grown for food include

   _____ and corn.

4. Crops are different from plants that

   _____ .

5. The natural resource of _____ is
   needed by all living things.

Label each group of words with a vocabulary word.

   cotton, rice, apples

1. _____

   oil, iron, clay

2. _____

# Make Connections

Read the paragraph below. Think about the meaning of each **bold** word. Then, check the Student Dictionary.

> The government of a state or country is based in a city called the **capital**. A **county** is an area with **local** government. A town or city called the county seat is the center for the county's government.

Underline the better ending to each sentence.

**1.** A county is part of a
   A. city.
   B. state.

**2.** The capital of the United States is
   A. Washington, D.C.
   B. the state of Washington.

**3.** A local event could take place
   A. throughout a country.
   B. in a neighborhood.

**4.** The state of Texas has many
   A. counties.
   B. capitals.

**5.** A leader of a local government is
   A. a mayor.
   B. a U.S. senator.

 **Challenge!**

Could a capital be a county seat? Write a reason for your answer.

_____

_____

# Make Connections

Read the paragraph below. Think about the meaning of each **bold** term. Then, check the Student Dictionary.

> The travelers climbed from the **valley** up eastern slopes that became steeper and steeper. At last, they reached the **mountain pass** that led to the other side. At the high **elevation**, they could see the western forests far below.

Circle *Yes* or *No* for each question. Write your reason on the line.

1. Is land at sea level at a high elevation?      Yes  No

_____

2. Is a valley always next to a mountain?      Yes  No

_____

3. Is a mountain pass like a passage?      Yes  No

_____

4. Could people live in a valley?      Yes  No

 **Word Alert!**

The words *elevator* and *elevation* are in the same word family. They have related meanings. Another word in the same family is underlined in the sentence below. Write a meaning for that word. Use what you know about the meanings of *elevator* and *elevation*.

We rode on an <u>elevated</u> train.

_____

# Make Connections

Read the paragraph below. Think about the meaning of each **bold** word. Then, check the Student Dictionary.

> Valleys, mountains, hills . . . how many **landforms** can you name? A **plain** is flat land with few trees. A **mesa** is also flat, but it is higher than the land below and has steep sides. A **cliff** is also high and steep. If you stand on the edge of a cliff, you will probably see water far below.

Complete each sentence with a vocabulary word from the paragraph above.

1. Waves splash against the base of the _____.

2. Drive on a highway in the southwestern United States, and you may see a _____ rising in the distance.

3. Cliffs, mesas, and plains are examples of _____.

4. A mesa is like a _____, because both are high landforms.

5. A plain is like a _____, because both have flat surfaces.

## Word Alert!

Homophones are words that sound alike but have different spellings and meanings. One of the vocabulary words is a homophone for *plane*. Write the vocabulary word on the blank to complete the sentence below. Then, tell what the sentence means in your own words.

The plane flew over the _____.

_____

# Make Connections

Read the paragraph below. Think about the meaning of each **bold** word. Then, check the Student Dictionary.

> Some people in **coastal** areas depend on fishing. The level of water in a **harbor** rises and falls with the **tides**, so the best time to set sail may be at high tide. Fishing boats return to the **port** to unload their catches.

Underline the better ending to each sentence.

1. A coastal region is never
   A. inland.
   B. an island.

2. A harbor could be
   A. deep or shallow.
   B. a river or a stream.

3. If you were on a beach at low tide, you would
   A. see few or no waves reach the shore.
   B. walk farther to reach the water's edge.

4. Coastal cities have ports where
   A. trading ships dock.
   B. airplanes land.

5. A harbor is like a
   A. port.
   B. tide.

6. You can tell from the names of the cities Portland, Portsmouth, and Greenport that the cities are
   A. by water.
   B. in cold climates.

# Make Connections

Read each pair of vocabulary words. Write the words where they fit in the sentences. Check the Student Dictionary for any meanings that you need.

1. kilometers          elevation

   Land that is five _____ above sea level is at a very high

   _____.

2. climate          coastal

   The ocean has a big effect on the _____ in

   _____ areas.

3. environment          local

   What are some living things in your _____

   _____?

4. natural resource          grassland

   Rich soil is a _____ in a well-watered

   _____.

5. landform          continent

   Mountains are a _____ on every _____.

6. crops          weather

   Farmers depend on good _____ to grow their

   _____.

Choose two of the vocabulary words on this page. Write them in a sentence. Then, write the sentence again on another sheet of paper. Leave blank lines for the two words. Challenge a partner to complete your sentence.

_____

_____

         *Words Every Third Grader Needs to Know!*

# Play With Words

## Code Words

Choose the word that fits in each sentence. Circle its letter.

1. The ___ of Canada is Ottawa.
   c  continent
   d  capital
   e  North America

2. A map is drawn to a ___.
   e  scale
   f  climate
   g  landform

3. An area of low land is a ___.
   q  cliff
   r  tide
   s  valley

4. A city might grow near a good ___.
   l  kilometer
   m  county
   e  harbor

5. A ___ is a high, flat landform.
   r  mesa
   s  plain
   t  mountain pass

6. North America is ___.
   s  an environment
   t  a continent
   u  a natural resource

Write the circled letters in order. You will find the name of a land in a dry climate.

_____

# Play With Words

## Vocabulary Search

Use each clue to find a vocabulary word in the puzzle. The words go across and down. Then, write the word below.

Clues

1. South America and Asia

2. Cold, windy, rainy ___

3. One thousand meters

4. By the seashore

5. Distance above sea level

6. A large, flat landform

7. Corn, wheat, oranges

8. A low land

```
G  O  P  A  B  R  D  I  H  T  M  L  C
E  S  U  L  O  C  F  P  W  E  Y  I  W
X  G  K  I  L  O  M  E  T  E  R  O  E
C  E  W  I  H  N  A  Q  U  I  A  D  A
E  L  E  V  A  T  I  O  N  O  H  F  T
U  B  I  O  E  I  G  U  P  J  I  O  H
E  N  A  L  O  N  D  E  M  C  N  T  E
I  O  C  E  F  E  J  A  B  O  X  M  R
Z  P  L  A  I  N  I  T  S  A  G  E  K
I  F  S  D  X  T  A  E  W  S  U  I  O
T  C  R  O  P  S  N  O  P  T  L  Z  V
K  O  W  E  R  T  S  S  B  A  R  G  D
F  A  N  C  H  I  V  A  L  L  E  Y  E
```

Answers

1. _____

2. _____

3. _____

4. _____

5. _____

6. _____

7. _____

8. _____

# Important Civics and Economics Words You Need to Know!

Use this list to keep track of how well you know the new words.

0 = Don't Know          1 = Know It Somewhat          2 = Know It Well

___ ___ authority

___ ___ barter

___ ___ budget

___ ___ citizenship

___ ___ civic responsibility

___ ___ civil rights

___ ___ common good

___ ___ consumer

___ ___ currency

___ ___ direct democracy

___ ___ duty

___ ___ economy

___ ___ exchange

___ ___ export

___ ___ federal

___ ___ illegal

___ ___ import

___ ___ income

___ ___ industry

___ ___ justice

___ ___ legal

___ ___ legislature

___ ___ manufacturing

___ ___ office

___ ___ producer

___ ___ profit

___ ___ public service

___ ___ represent

___ ___ representative democracy

___ ___ tolerance

# Explore a Word

Follow these steps.

**1.** Read the sentence below. Think about the meaning of the **bold** word.

> "We have been treated unfairly," said the leader of the group. "We demand **justice**!"

**2.** What do you think the word means? Write your idea.

**justice:** _____

_____

**3.** Write a sentence with the word **justice**. Show what it means.

_____

_____

**4.** Check the meaning of **justice** in the Student Dictionary.

**5.** If your sentence in step 3 matches the meaning, put a ✓ after it. If your sentence does not match the meaning, write a better sentence.

_____

_____

**6.** Make a simple drawing to show the meaning of **justice**.

# Explore a Word

Read the sentences below. Think about the meaning of the **bold** word. Then, check the Student Dictionary.

> One person's beliefs may be the opposite of another person's beliefs. But the two people get along if they show **tolerance**.
>
> Americans are free to practice any religion they choose. A government shows religious tolerance by not interfering with people's choices.

Fill out the web to show your ideas about tolerance.

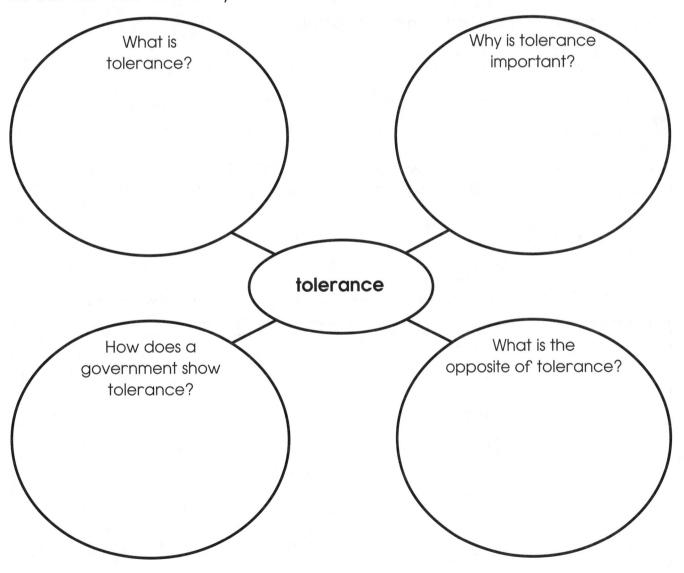

# Compare Words

Read the sentences. Think about the meaning of each **bold** word. Then, check the Student Dictionary.

> It's **legal** to cross a street at a crosswalk. It's **illegal** to drop litter on the sidewalk.

Read each sentence. Is the action legal or illegal? Circle the answer.

1. Mayra unbuckles her seatbelt in a moving car.   legal   illegal

2. Matt keeps his dog on a leash in the park.   legal   illegal

3. Sonia rides her bike on a bike path.   legal   illegal

4. A big crowd gathers to hear a speech.   legal   illegal

5. A gas station leaks oil into a river.   legal   illegal

6. A child pulls a fire alarm when there is no fire.   legal   illegal

## Word Alert!

A prefix is a word part added before a base word. The prefixes *il-*, *im-*, and *in-* can mean "not." Write a meaning for each word below. Use the base word in your meaning.

1. illegal: _____

2. imperfect: _____

3. incomplete: _____

# Compare Words

Read the paragraph. Think about the meaning of each **bold** word. Then, check the Student Dictionary.

> United States farmers grow soybeans that other countries want to buy. Soybeans are a major U.S. **export**. The United States does not grow much coffee, so it **imports** coffee from other countries.

Circle the word that completes each sentence.

1. An (import/export) is a product that comes into a country from the country where it was made.

2. Farmers grow crops that are (imported/exported) to foreign lands.

3. A country must (import/export) oil if it does not have enough oil of its own.

4. Factories might buy (imported/exported) metals to use in making new products.

5. China makes and (imports/exports) more products to the United States than the United States sells to China.

##  Challenge!

Imports and exports have to do with the balance of trade between two countries. What do you think *balance of trade* means? Draw a picture to show its meaning. Use the words *imports* and *exports* in your drawing.

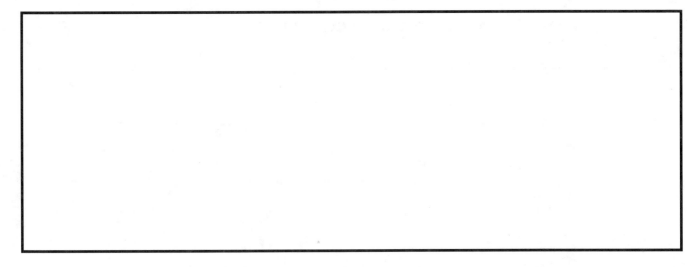

# Compare Words

Read the paragraph below. Think about the meaning of each **bold** word. Then, check the Student Dictionary.

> When was the last time you were a **consumer**? It might have been today, if you spent any money. Anyone who buys a product is a consumer. A consumer also buys services, such as a haircut or car wash. The businesses that make products or provide services are called **producers**.

Follow each instruction.

**1.** Name two producers who provide services.

_____

**2.** Name two things that factories produce.

_____

**3.** Circle the word that is a synonym for *consumer* in the sentence below.

The customer purchased a box of fruit.

**4.** Complete the sentence below with your own idea.

Producers want consumers to _____

_____

**5.** Explain what the sentence below means in your own words.

At times, a producer is also a consumer.

_____

# Make Connections

Read the sentence below. Think about the meaning of each **bold** word. Then, check the Student Dictionary.

> The U.S. President is elected to **office** for a four-year term. The President has the **authority** to name people who will hold other offices, such as the Secretary of Defense or the Secretary of Education.

Complete each sentence with your own idea.

1. A school has an office. But that kind of office is different from the kind of office that someone holds. The difference is _____

   _____

2. Students do not have the authority to change school rules. The people with that authority are _____

   _____

3. Voters elect a leader to a government office. They give that person the authority to _____

   _____

4. Citizens may want to meet with someone who holds an office of authority in government. The reason for the meeting might be _____

   _____

 **Word Alert!**

Read the sentence below to find three words from the same word family. Write the three words on the line.

The governor's office gave official orders to the officers of the state police.

_____

# Make Connections

Read the sentence below. Think about the meaning of each **bold** word. Then, check the Student Dictionary.

> A person, a family, and a government all earn **income**. Their **budgets** show how they will use the income to pay for the things they need.

Underline the better ending to each sentence.

1. Most people get their income from
   A. their jobs.
   B. their travels.

2. A government gets its income from
   A. taxes.
   B. producers.

3. A family's budget must include
   A. the cost of food.
   B. the selling of services.

4. A budget helps a person
   A. keep an eye on spending.
   B. earn more money at work.

5. If someone doesn't have enough money to buy something right now, a budget can help the person
   A. use a credit card to borrow money.
   B. set aside some income as savings.

6. An item likely to be listed in a person's budget is
   A. clothing.
   B. friendship.

# Make Connections

Read the sentences below. Think about the meaning of each **bold** term. Then, check the Student Dictionary.

> "Thank you for electing me," said the mayor to the people of the city. "I have worked in **public service** my whole life. And I intend to keep working for the **common good**."

Complete each sentence with one or more words that make sense.

1. City _____ are a public service that people use for transportation.

2. Workers who provide public services include teachers, firefighters, and _____.

3. The common good _____ all the members of a group.

4. A government _____ for the common good.

5. A public service such as _____ is provided for the common good.

6. Taxpayers _____ the public services that everyone uses.

# Make Connections

Read the paragraph below. Think about the meaning of each **bold** word. Then, check the Student Dictionary.

> Businesses in every **industry** try to make a **profit**. For example, the **manufacturing** of sneakers costs money. To make a profit, the factory owners must sell their sneakers for more money than they paid to make them.

Underline the better ending to each sentence.

1. An example of an industry is
   A. making a profit.
   B. building houses.

2. Most manufacturing takes place in
   A. factories.
   B. schools.

3. To make a profit, a business must
   A. spend more than it earns.
   B. earn more than it spends.

4. Examples of manufactured products are
   A. stoves and sinks.
   B. fire and water.

5. Fishing, mining, and transportation are all
   A. industries.
   B. manufacturers.

6. If a toy store does not make a profit,
   A. toy manufacturing will grow.
   B. the store might have to close.

# Make Connections

Read the paragraph below. Think about the meaning of each **bold** word. Then, check the Student Dictionary.

> Imagine an **economy** in which there was no such thing as money. In an economy based on **barter**, a farmer might barter vegetables for cloth woven by a traveling weaver. The invention of **currency** meant that the farmer could **exchange** vegetables for coins or paper money. Then, the farmer could use the money to buy cloth and other products.

Complete each sentence with a vocabulary word from the paragraph above.

1. The U.S. dollar is a kind of _____.

2. A growing _____ means more jobs and more profits for businesses.

3. A big problem with _____ is that someone with a product that you want might not be willing to trade with you.

4. The _____ of goods and services is part of every economy.

5. Japanese units of currency are called *yen*. Americans traveling in Japan would _____ U.S. dollars for yen.

 ## Look It Up!

How can you find the names of currencies used throughout the world? A dictionary lists each name. Some dictionaries also give a table of currencies with the entry *currency*. Play a dictionary game with a partner to match a currency to its country or countries. Here are some currencies to start with: *yen, euro, pound, peso, ruble, rupee, dinar*.

# Make Connections

Read the paragraph below. Think about the meaning of each **bold** term. Then, check the Student Dictionary.

> Citizens want a government that respects their **civil rights**. **Citizenship** brings rights, but it also brings **duties**. Citizens show **civic responsibility** in many ways. One important way is by voting. Civic responsibilities also include obeying laws and staying informed about government matters.

Circle *Yes* or *No* for each question. Write your reason on the line.

**1.** Are civil rights like human rights?                         Yes   No

_____

**2.** Do students your age have any duties?                  Yes   No

_____

**3.** Is paying taxes a civic responsibility?                 Yes   No

_____

**4.** Do civil rights have to do with war?                    Yes   No

_____

**5.** Are Americans the only people with citizenship?    Yes   No

_____

*Words Every Third Grader Needs to Know!*

# Make Connections

Read the paragraph below. Think about the meaning of each **bold** term. Then, check the Student Dictionary.

> The United States has a **federal** system of government. Each state in the union gives certain powers to the central government. The U.S. government is also a **representative democracy**. Voters elect members of the **legislature** to **represent** citizens' interests. A representative democracy is different from a **direct democracy**, in which the citizens vote on laws themselves.

Complete each sentence with your own idea.

1. In a representative democracy, citizens do not govern themselves directly. Instead, they _____

   _____

2. A state has its own government. But the federal government can tell

   _____

   _____

3. The members of a legislature try to decide _____

   _____

4. Voters choose a person to represent them. The voters believe that the person will _____

   _____

5. A direct democracy is not a good system for governing millions of people. There would be problems because _____

   _____

# Make Connections

Read each pair of vocabulary words. Write the words where they fit in the sentences. Check the Student Dictionary for any meanings that you need.

1. exports          economy

   A country's _____ to other countries are part of its

   _____ .

2. federal          budget

   People pay taxes to the _____ government. The

   government's use of tax money is shown in its _____ .

3. justice          authority

   Judges have the _____ to make decisions about

   _____ .

4. represent          common good

   The state senator will _____ thousands of people in her

   district and work for their _____ .

5. legislature          illegal

   It is _____ to ride a bike without a helmet. Our state

   _____ passed a law requiring the wearing of helmets.

Write a sentence with the vocabulary words *producer* and *consumer*. Then, write the sentence again with blanks instead of the words. Challenge a partner to complete your sentence.

_____

_____

# Play With Words

## Code Words

Choose the word that fits in each sentence. Circle its letter.

1. Trash collection is ___.
   - **p** a public service
   - **q** a civil right
   - **r** an import

2. The members of a legislature ___ citizens.
   - **q** direct democracy
   - **r** represent
   - **s** office

3. Trading a service for goods is ___.
   - **n** illegal
   - **o** barter
   - **p** industry

4. A dollar is a unit of ___.
   - **d** budget
   - **e** economy
   - **f** currency

5. ___ produces goods.
   - **h** A consumer
   - **i** Manufacturing
   - **j** An import

6. ___ includes goods and services.
   - **t** An economy
   - **b** Citizenship
   - **c** Civic responsibility

Write the circled letters in order. You will find a word that answers this question: *What is a business owner's goal?*

_____

# Play With Words

## Hidden Message

Read the clue. Find and circle the vocabulary word that matches the clue.

1. Respect for others' views
2. A user of a product
3. ___ rights
4. U.S. voters have this.
5. Lawful
6. The U.S. Congress

t h t o l e r a n c e e m o r
e y o u t c o n s u m e r a k
e f r o c i v i l m i t t h e b
i g g e c i t i z e n s h i p r i t
g e t s w h l e g a l a t i s
i t a h l e g i s l a t u r e o l e

Look back to find the letters you did NOT circle. Write them in order on the lines below to find a riddle and its answer.

— — —   — — — —   — — —   — — — —

— — — —   — —,   — — —   — — — — — —

— —   — — — —.   — — — —   — —   — —?

(— — — — — — —)

# Important Art Words You Need to Know!

Use this list to keep track of how well you know the new words.

0 = Don't Know      I = Know It Somewhat      2 = Know It Well

___ ___ animation

___ ___ ballet

___ ___ chord

___ ___ chorus

___ ___ cityscape

___ ___ concert

___ ___ cool colors

___ ___ duet

___ ___ horizontal

___ ___ landscape

___ ___ melody

___ ___ performance

___ ___ position

___ ___ quartet

___ ___ seascape

___ ___ still life

___ ___ tempo

___ ___ trio

___ ___ vertical

___ ___ warm colors

# Explore a Word

Follow these steps.

1. Read the sentence below. Think about the meaning of the **bold** word.

> Artists use computers to make **animations** that look like real-life movement.

2. What do you think the word means? Write your idea.

**animation:** _____

_____

3. Write a sentence with the word **animation**. Show what it means.

_____

_____

4. Check the meaning of **animation** in the Student Dictionary.

5. If your sentence in step 3 matches the meaning, put a ✓ after it. If your sentence does not match the meaning, write a better sentence.

_____

_____

6. Make a simple drawing to show the meaning of **animation**.

# Explore a Word

Read the sentence below. Think about the meaning of the **bold** word.
Then, check the Student Dictionary.

> The audience cheered and clapped during the dance **performance**.

Fill out this web to show your ideas about performances.

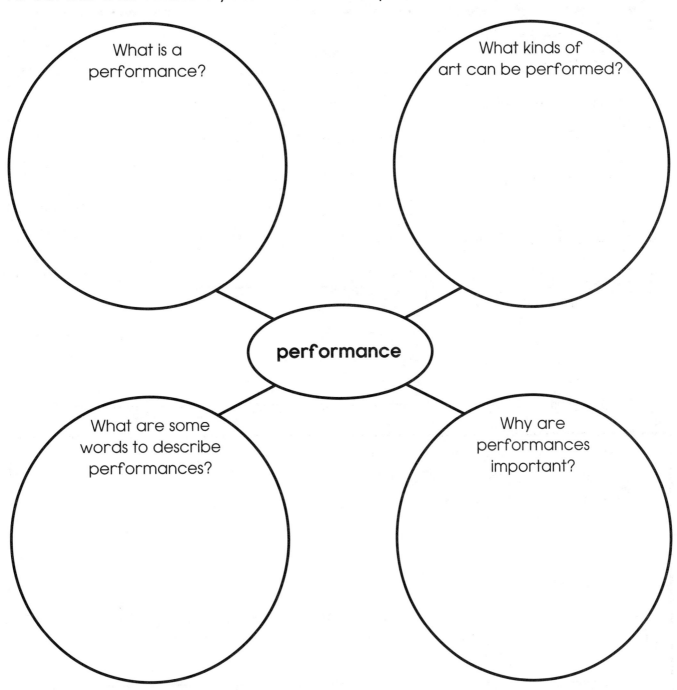

What is a
performance?

What kinds of
art can be performed?

**performance**

What are some
words to describe
performances?

Why are
performances
important?

# Compare Words

Read the paragraph below. Think about the meaning of each **bold** word. Then, check the Student Dictionary.

> Hold your arms out to your sides as far as they will stretch. The imaginary line between your hands is **horizontal**. Picture a line from the top of your head to your feet. That imaginary line is **vertical**.

Follow each instruction.

1. In the box, draw a capital letter *T*. Write *vertical* and *horizontal* to label the lines in it.

2. Write a capital letter that has one vertical line and three horizontal lines. _____

3. Name two horizontal shapes you see around you.

   _____

4. Name two vertical shapes you see around you.

   _____

5. Draw a pattern of horizontal and vertical lines. Make it interesting by varying the thickness of the lines and the size of the spaces.

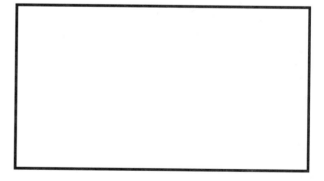

 **Look It Up!**

Look up *horizon* in a classroom dictionary. Draw or write to show how it is related in meaning to *horizontal*.

_____

# Compare Words

Read the paragraph below. Think about the meaning of each **bold** word. Then, check the Student Dictionary.

> The artist used **cool colors** to show water and **warm colors** to show the setting sun. The water is blue-green, and the sky is pink-orange.

Read each sentence. Does it tell about a warm color or a cool color? Circle the answer.

1. A log is burning in the fireplace.          warm color     cool color

2. A yellow sun is overhead.          warm color     cool color

3. The trees have dark green leaves.          warm color     cool color

4. The sky is bright blue.          warm color     cool color

5. Blue-purple plums fill the bowl.          warm color     cool color

6. The glass is filled with orange juice.          warm color     cool color

7. Red tulips grow against a fence.          warm color     cool color

8. Green ferns grow by a stream.          warm color     cool color

# Make Connections

Read the sentence below. Think about the meaning of each **bold** word. Then, check the Student Dictionary.

> Children begin their study of **ballet** by learning the five basic **positions** of the feet.

Complete each sentence with one or more words that make sense.

1. In any form of dance, the positions of the _____ _____ and feet are important.

2. Special shoes help a ballet dancer _____ on the tips of her toes.

3. Ballet dancers train hard to make _____ and spins look easy.

4. A ballet dancer is able to position _____ so that the foot points to the ceiling.

5. Ballet dancers change their positions as they listen _____.

 **Challenge!**

The word *ballet* comes from French, because France was home to schools of ballet long ago. To this day, ballet terms are French. Find a person who has studied ballet. Ask for three ballet terms. Then, use a dictionary to try to find the spellings of those terms.

Name _____

# Make Connections

Read the paragraph below. Think about the meaning of each **bold** term. Then, check the Student Dictionary.

> A **trio** of musicians played a song. A fourth musician joined in, and the **quartet** played together. Then, a man and a woman came onstage to sing a **duet**.

Underline the better ending to each sentence.

1. A duet may be performed by
   A. two musicians.
   B. three singers.

2. A singing trio has
   A. exactly three singers.
   B. at least three singers.

3. A quartet could include
   A. two singers and four musicians.
   B. two violins, a viola, and a cello.

4. The singers of a duet
   A. perform alone and together.
   B. must be male and female.

5. The difference between a trio and a quartet is
   A. a trio has one more performer.
   B. a quartet has one more performer.

## 🔍 Word Alert!

One of the vocabulary words has the number prefix *tri-*. Read the list of words below. Underline the prefix *tri-* in each. Then, tell how all the words are alike in meaning.

| triangle | trio | triple | tricycle | triplet |
|----------|------|--------|----------|---------|

_____

_____

*Words Every Third Grader Needs to Know!*                                    111

# Make Connections

Read the paragraph below. Think about the meaning of each **bold** word. Then, check the Student Dictionary.

> Some paintings and drawings are **still lifes**. In a still life, an artist shows objects that are not moving. A still life is usually set indoors. Outdoor scenes are shown in **landscapes** or **seascapes** of the natural world. A **cityscape** shows streets and buildings.

Read the title of each painting. Imagine what the painting looks like. Write the vocabulary word that names the kind of painting.

1. "Three Lemons in a Glass Bowl"        _____

2. "Ocean Bay at Sunset"        _____

3. "Green Buses on Silver Bridge"        _____

4. "Forest Waterfall"        _____

5. "View From Rocky Hill"        _____

# Challenge!

Choose one of the paintings from the list above. Make a sketch to show what you would include in a painting with that title. Use another sheet of paper if necessary.

# Make Connections

Read the paragraph below. Think about the meaning of each **bold** word. Then, check the Student Dictionary.

> The teacher played a few **chords** on the piano. Then, she played a **melody** while the **chorus** sang along. The song began at a slow **tempo** but became faster and livelier. The chorus is getting ready for a **concert** for students, teachers, and parents.

Circle *Yes* or *No* for each question. Write your reason on the line.

**1.** Can a chorus have just one person?                                     Yes   No

_____

**2.** Could someone hum a chord?                                            Yes   No

_____

**3.** Is a melody the same as a note?                                       Yes   No

_____

**4.** Does a tempo have to do with speed?                                   Yes   No

_____

**5.** Is a concert like a performance?                                      Yes   No

_____

# Make Connections

Read each pair of vocabulary words. Write the words where they fit in the sentences. Check the Student Dictionary for any meanings that you need.

1. position          animation

   The art of _____ involves changing the

   _____ of something so that it seems to move.

2. tempo          ballet

   The _____ dancers whirled to the speedy

   _____ of the music.

3. vertical          landscape

   The painter used many _____ shapes to show tall trees

   in the _____.

4. concert          quartet

   The four singers in the _____ gave a _____

   at the town hall.

5. duet          chorus

   Two members of the _____ stepped forward to sing a

   _____.

Write your own sentence with the vocabulary words *trio* and *performance*. Then, write the sentence again with blanks instead of the words. Challenge a partner to complete your sentence.

_____

_____

# Play With Words

## Code Words

Choose the word that fits in each sentence. Circle its letter.

1. Several notes played at once make a ___.
   - **a** melody
   - **b** chord
   - **c** chorus

2. A drawing of an outdoor scene could be a ___.
   - **c** vertical
   - **d** still life
   - **e** cityscape

3. Light blue is a ___.
   - **a** cool color
   - **b** warm color
   - **c** tempo

4. A tune is also called a ___.
   - **s** chord
   - **t** duet
   - **u** melody

5. The ocean meets the sky in a ___ line.
   - **t** horizontal
   - **u** vertical
   - **v** seascape

6. A painting of books on a table is a ___.
   - **w** performance
   - **x** position
   - **y** still life

Write the circled letters in order. You will find a word that answers this question: *What do artists often think about?*

_____

# Play With Words

## Vocabulary Search

Use each clue to find a vocabulary word in the puzzle. The words go across and down. Then, write the word below.

Clues

1. Red and orange are ___ colors.
2. Duet, ___, quartet
3. A cartoon
4. A group of singers

5. A synonym for *concert*
6. From top to bottom
7. A painting of water
8. First ___ in ballet

| I | B | L | W | A | R | M | I | E | F | U | H | M |
|---|---|---|---|---|---|---|---|---|---|---|---|---|
| A | D | E | H | N | P | A | R | O | X | I | Y | S |
| O | P | O | S | I | T | I | O | N | D | W | A | G |
| K | A | E | J | M | I | A | S | B | V | O | N | W |
| E | P | U | T | A | L | E | T | O | E | F | U | A |
| A | D | M | B | T | R | I | O | E | R | Q | P | R |
| F | N | E | R | I | A | C | I | V | T | U | S | K |
| A | O | L | H | O | N | S | E | G | I | Y | A | O |
| V | E | I | U | N | S | E | A | S | C | A | P | E |
| Y | A | P | E | R | F | O | R | M | A | N | C | E |
| C | H | O | R | U | S | O | E | D | L | Z | I | C |
| R | U | T | I | U | X | A | L | Z | E | W | T | M |
| E | C | O | G | N | E | J | I | B | P | O | A | H |

Answers

1. _____
2. _____
3. _____
4. _____

5. _____
6. _____
7. _____
8. _____

# Game Ideas and Suggestions

Use games and activities to help students better hear, see, and remember content-area vocabulary words. The suggestions on these pages can be used with the words in this book and with any other vocabulary words that students are learning.

## Charades

Choose about ten vocabulary words. Write the words on slips of paper and display them. Give students time to think about the words before removing the slips. Then, divide the group into two teams. One team member chooses a slip, holds up fingers to indicate the number of syllables, and pantomimes the word. Teammates try to guess the word within a certain time limit.

## Word Art

Help students select vocabulary words to depict as art. Encourage them to use letter shapes and arrangements to indicate what the words mean. Prompt students with questions, such as "How might you arrange the letters of the word *valley*?" Or "What might happen to the letters in *evaporate*?"

## Vocabulary Word-O

Reproduce and distribute the Word-O game card on page 119 to each student. Write 20 vocabulary words on slips of paper, and display the slips. Have students choose 9 words to write on their cards. Shuffle the slips, and choose one slip at a time. Instead of reading the word aloud, offer a clue about it. For example, for the word *numerator*, you might start with the content area. "This is a math word having to do with fractions." Or use a strong context sentence, with "blank" for the word. "In the fraction three-fourths, three is the 'blank.'" Students should check off the word if it is on their grids. The first student to complete three across, down, or diagonally calls out "Word-O" and reads aloud the three words.

## Connect a Word

Have students name a vocabulary word for you to write on the board. Draw a box around the word. Then, randomly choose another vocabulary word, and write it in a box to the right of the first word. Have individuals or partners take turns trying to come up with a sentence that contains both words. If the group agrees that the sentence makes sense (even if it is silly), draw an arrow between the boxes to connect them. To make the game more challenging, use vocabulary words from different content areas.

## Card Pairs

Use index cards cut in half to prepare a deck of 52 cards. Write 26 vocabulary words and 26 synonyms or short definitions on the cards. The cards can be used in a variety of games, such as Memory or Concentration. Below is one suggestion.

- **Go Fish!** for 2 to 5 Players
- Each player is dealt five cards. The remaining cards are placed face down in a pile.

- The player to the right of the dealer starts by setting aside any pairs. Then, he or she asks the player on the right for a card needed to make a pair. "Do you have *antonym*?" Or "Do you have the meaning of *antonym*?"

- If the holder has the requested card, he or she hands it over. If the holder does not have it, the player must "go fish" and draw the top card from the pile. If no match can be made, the next player takes a turn.

- The winner is the first player with no cards in hand or the player with the most pairs after all cards have been drawn.

## Word Hunt

Emphasize that vocabulary words appear in print and online in a variety of informational resources. As you come across a vocabulary word—in a headline, news article, advertisement, or another resource—save the printed source or make a printout. Challenge students to read the text to find the vocabulary word and to explain what it means in the provided context.

## Dictionary Guess

Have one student randomly choose a word from the Student Dictionary and read the definition aloud to the group. Partners or small groups then try to write the vocabulary word that matches the definition. Continue until each student has had a chance to choose a word and read its definition aloud. A point is awarded for each correct word.

## Racetrack Games

Have students design their own racetrack board games or make one from a template you provide, such as the template on page 120. Here is one way to use the template.

- Select 20 vocabulary words for students to write in the spaces.

- Make a small cardboard spinner by drawing a circle divided into three sections labeled, 1, 2, and 3. The "spinner" can be a paper clip attached to a paper fastener.

- Provide small objects for students to use as markers.

- Each player spins, and the highest number goes first.

- A player spins and moves the marker the number of spaces shown. The player must say the word on the space and demonstrate knowledge of it by giving its definition or using it in a good context sentence.

- Players may use a dictionary to check the player's response. A player who is not correct loses a turn.

- The first player to reach the finish line wins.

| OI | RD | WO |
|---|---|---|
| | | |
| | | |
| | | |

**Finish**

**Start**

_____'s

# Student Dictionary

# Important Math Words I Need to Know!

**angle** (ANG gul) *noun* The space between two lines that meet at an endpoint, or the space between two flat surfaces that meet at a line.

**area** (AIR ee uh) *noun* The number of square units that fill a surface. *The bedroom has an area of 120 square feet.*

**decimal point** (DES ih mul point) *noun* The dot in a number that separates whole numbers from tenths, hundredths, thousandths, and so on. A decimal point separates dollars from cents in written amounts of money.

**denominator** (dih NOM ih nay ter) *noun* The number below the line in a fraction. The denominator tells how many equal parts the whole has been broken into.

**diagonal** (dy AG nul) *noun* A slanted line that connects opposite corners.

**digit** (DIJ it) *noun* One of the numbers 0 through 9.

**division** (dih VIZH un) *noun* Figuring out how many times one amount can fit into another amount; the act of dividing. *We used division to split 45 crayons evenly among three friends.*

**equilateral triangle** (EE kwuh lat ur ul TRY ang gul) or (EK wuh lat er ul) *noun* A triangle with three sides of equal length.

**fraction** (FRAK shun) *noun* A part of a whole. *Add the fractions $\frac{1}{2}$ and $\frac{1}{2}$ to get 1.*

**hexagon** (HEK suh gon) *noun* A flat shape with six sides. A hexagon may have six sides of equal lengths or of different lengths.

**line segment** (line SEG mint) *noun* All the points on a straight path from one endpoint to another endpoint, including both endpoints.

**measurement** (MEZH ur mint) *noun* The use of standard units to tell length, size, weight, amount, time, and so on. *Meter sticks, tablespoons, and balance scales are three tools used for measurement.*

**multiple** (MUL tuh pul) *noun* A number that can be divided evenly by a particular number. *The number 3 has the multiples 6, 9, 12, 15, and so on.*

**multiplication** (mul tuh plih KAY shun) *noun* Adding a number to itself two or more times; the act of multiplying. *We used multiplication to figure out how many crayons we needed in order to give 5 crayons to each of 25 children.*

**numerator** (NOO mur ay tur) *noun* The number above the line in a fraction. The numerator tells how many parts of the whole are noted.

**octagon** (OK tuh gon) *noun* A flat shape with eight sides. An octagon may have eight sides of equal lengths or of different lengths.

**pentagon** (PEN tuh gon) *noun* A flat shape with five sides. A pentagon may have five sides of equal lengths or of different lengths.

**perimeter** (puh RIM uh tur) *noun* The distance around the outside of a flat shape.

**perpendicular** (pur pin DIK yuh lur) *adjective* Describing two lines that cross at right angles, one going left and right, and the other going up and down.

*Words Every Third Grader Needs to Know!*

*The top edge and the side edge of a sheet of paper are perpendicular.*

**polygon** (POL ee gon) *noun* A flat shape formed by three or more line segments. *Triangles, squares, and octagons are examples of polygons.*

**product** (PROD ukt) *noun* The answer in a multiplication problem. *Multiply 10 times 10 to get the product of 100.*

**quotient** (KWOH shunt) *noun* The answer in a division problem. *Divide 100 by 10 to get the quotient of 10.*

**rectangle** (REK tang gul) *noun* A flat shape with four sides and four right angles. *A square is a rectangle with four equal sides.*

**remainder** (rih MAYN dur) *noun* The number left over when a number is not divided evenly. *If two friends divide 9 candies, each friend will have 4 candies and there will be a remainder of 1.*

**right triangle** (rite TRY ang gul) *noun* A triangle with two sides that meet to form a right angle. A right angle is 90 degrees and is formed by two perpendicular lines.

# More Math Words I Need to Know:

_____

_____

_____

_____

_____

_____

_____

_____

_____

_____

_____

_____

_____

# Important Science and Health Words I Need to Know!

**adaptation** (ad ap TAY shun) *noun* A body part or a behavior that allows a life form to live in an environment. *Webbed feet are an adaptation that helps ducks swim.*

**asteroid** (AS tuh roid) *noun* A rock that is in orbit around the Sun. An asteroid is smaller than a planet.

**astronomer** (uh STRON uh mur) *noun* A scientist who studies space and the bodies in it.

**axis** (AK sis) *noun* An imaginary line that cuts through a planet. The planet spins around the line. *Earth spins on an axis through the North and South Poles.*

**carnivore** (KAR nih vor) *noun* **1.** An animal that eats other animals. **2.** A member of a group of meat-eating mammals that includes dogs, cats, and bears.

**comet** (KOM it) *noun* An icy body in space that has a long tail of gas and dust. In the solar system, comets take a long orbit around the Sun. *Halley's Comet can be seen as it nears the Sun about every 76 years.*

**condense** (kun DENS) *verb* To change from a gas into a liquid. *Drops of water condense on a bathroom mirror after you take a hot shower.*

**decomposer** (dee kum POH zur) *noun* A life form that breaks down the remains of dead plants and animals into simple nutrients that return to the soil to nourish plants. Most decomposers are bacteria and fungi.

**ecosystem** (EK oh sis tim) *noun* A community of living things along with the nonliving things in a natural area. *Scientists study how the sun's energy flows from plants to other living things in an ecosystem.*

**evaporate** (ih VAP uh rayt) *verb* To change from a liquid to a gas. *As the air heated up, the puddles on the street evaporated.*

**extinct** (ek STINKT) *adjective* No longer existing. A species is extinct when there are no more living members.

**food web** *noun* The network of connections among plants, animals that eat plants, and animals that eat plant-eaters. Diagrams of food webs have arrows showing how energy flows from the things that are eaten to the eaters.

**gas** *noun* A state of matter without a definite shape. The tiniest particles, or atoms, of the gas spread out to fill any space. *People breathe out the gas called carbon dioxide.*

**habitat** (HAB ih tat) *noun* The natural area in which a plant or an animal lives. *A stream is a habitat for beavers.*

**herbivore** (HER bih vor) *noun* An animal that feeds mainly on plants.

**humidity** (hyoo MID ih tee) *noun* The amount of moisture in the air. *Summer days with high humidity feel steamy.*

**liquid** (LIH kwid) *noun* A state of matter that changes shape and takes up a definite amount of space. The tiniest particles of the matter, or its atoms, are arranged more loosely than in a solid but more tightly than in a gas.

**matter** (MAT ur) *noun* Anything that can be weighed and takes up space.

**nutrient** (NOO tree int) *noun* A substance

that nourishes, or feeds, living things. *Water and proteins are basic nutrients for human bodies.*

**overheat** (oh vur HEET) *verb* To become too hot.

**orbit** (OR bit) *noun* The path that a planet or other body takes around a star, or the path that a moon takes around its planet. *verb* To take a path around a body in space.

**perspire** (pur SPIRE) *verb* To get rid of water through small holes, or pores, in the skin; to sweat.

**precipitation** (prih sip ih TAY shun) *noun* A form of water that falls to the Earth's surface. Rain, hail, snow, and sleet are precipitation.

**predator** (PRED uh tur) *noun* An animal that hunts and eats other animals.

**prey** (pray) *noun* Animals that are hunted and eaten by other animals. *Rabbits must be alert and fast to avoid becoming prey.*

**producer** (pruh DOO sur) *noun* A life form that uses the sun's energy and nonliving substances to make its own food. Green plants are producers that other living things depend on.

**reproduce** (REE pruh doos) *verb* To make more living things of the same kind. *Birds reproduce by making eggs.*

**revolve** (rih VOLV) *verb* To take a circular path around a central object. *Planets revolve around the Sun.*

**rotate** (ROH tayt) *verb* To turn like a wheel around a central point or line.

**solar system** (SOH lur SIS tim) *noun* The Sun and all the bodies that revolve around it. Planets, their moons, and comets are some of the bodies in our solar system.

**solid** (SOL id) *noun* A state of matter that has a definite shape and takes up a certain amount of space. The tiniest particles of the matter, or its atoms, are arranged more tightly in a solid than in a liquid or a gas.

**species** (SPEE sheez) *noun* A grouping of life forms in which all the members look like one another and can produce offspring together. *Scientists are still naming new species of plants and insects.*

**tilt** *verb* To slant. *Earth tilts to one side as it travels around the Sun.*

**water cycle** (WAH tur SY kul]) *noun* The never-ending changes that water goes through as it moves throughout the Earth. Water evaporates from bodies of water, rises into the sky as a gas, and then condenses to a liquid to fall back to the surface.

**water vapor** (WAH tur VAY per) *noun* Water in the form of a gas.

# More Science and Health Words I Need to Know:

_____

_____

_____

# Important Technology Words I Need to Know!

**brainstorm** (BRAYN storm) *verb* To think of ideas to solve problems, usually by talking in a group.

**browser** (BROU zur) *noun* A computer program that locates and shows information from the Internet and other networks.

**engineer** (EN jin eer) *noun* A person who uses science to design, plan, and build machines, buildings, products, and other technologies.

**force** (fors) *noun* A push or a pull. Forces cause objects to move, stop moving, or stay in place.

**gear** (geer) *noun* A simple machine that is made of at least two toothed wheels that turn together. The wheels may be connected directly or with a belt that moves between them.

**Internet** (IN tur net) *noun* The worldwide network that connects computer networks. The Internet connects a computer to email, the World Wide Web, and other services.

**inventor** (in VENT ur) *noun* Someone who uses science and imagination to plan something that has never been made before.

**model** (MOD ul) *noun* A first example of a new machine, device, or other product. A model is used to test how well the product works and what needs to be improved.

**pulley** (PUL ee) *noun* A simple machine that is made of a wheel with a grooved rim for a rope or a belt. Pulling on one end of the rope lifts an object on the other end.

**ramp** *noun* A simple machine that is made of a sloping surface. A ramp is also called an *inclined plane*.

**recycle** (ree SY kul) *verb* To take out useful materials from things that are thrown away and find new uses for those materials. *We fill bins with paper and plastic so that they will be recycled into new products.*

**reduce** (rih DOOS) *verb* To lower the amount of something. *We reduced our use of paper by writing on both sides of every sheet.*

**reuse** (ree YOOZ) *verb* To use again. *Instead of throwing out paper bags, we reuse them as book covers.*

**simple machine** (SIM pul muh SHEEN) *noun* One of the six basic machines that are used alone or as part of other machines to make work easier. Simple machines have no or few moving parts. The six simple machines are the ramp, pulley, wheel and axle, gear, wedge, lever, and screw.

**wheel and axle** (WEEL and AK sul) *noun* A simple machine that is made of a rod, called an *axle*, attached to the center of a wheel. Turning the axle causes the wheel to turn. Or, turning the wheel causes the axle to turn.

---

# More Technology Words I Need to Know:

_____

_____

_____

_____

_____

_____

_____

_____

_____

_____

_____

_____

_____

_____

_____

_____

_____

_____

# Important Language Arts Words I Need to Know!

**adjective** (AJ ik tiv) *noun* A word that describes a noun. *Examples: round, sweet, hard candy.*

**antonym** (AN tuh nim) *noun* A word with an opposite meaning. *The words* hot *and* cold *are antonyms.*

**biography** (by OG ruh fee) *noun* The true story of a person's life.

**context clue** (KON tekst kloo) *noun* An idea in the words around an unknown word, which point to the meaning of the unknown word.

**definition** (def ih NIH shun) *noun* The meaning of a word.

**dialogue** (DY uh log) *noun* The words spoken by characters in a story.

**draft** *noun* An early form of a written work. *verb* To write the first form of a work.

**fact** (fakt) *noun* A piece of information that is true and can be proved.

**fantasy** (FAN tuh see) *noun* A fiction story in which things happen that could never happen in real life. *The children flew to the Moon on the back of a winged horse in this fantasy.*

**fiction** (FIK shun) *noun* A story that is made up by the author.

**haiku** (HY koo) *noun* A three-line poem with a syllable pattern of 5-7-5 and no rhyme. The poem is usually about nature. Haiku are based on a Japanese form of poetry.

**homophone** (HOM uh fone) *noun* A word that sounds like another word but has a different spelling and meaning. *The words* rain, rein, *and* reign *are homophones.*

**index** (IN deks) *noun* A part of a book that lists topics in the book and gives the pages where information can be found. An index is usually in the back of the book. *The index to the book about dinosaurs lists ten pages of information about their eating habits.*

**inference** (IN fur ins) *noun* An idea that a reader can figure out even though it is not directly stated by the author. *The little boy in the story hides whenever visitors come to the house, so I made the inference that he is shy.*

**journal** (JUR nul) *noun* A daily record of experiences and thoughts. *Some writers share their journals, but others keep them private.*

**nonfiction** (non FIK shun) *noun* A true story or other written work that gives information. Nonfiction is about things that really happened and does not come from the author's imagination. Science books, history books, and biographies are examples of nonfiction.

**noun** *noun* A word that names a person, place, or thing. *Examples: mother, country, book.*

**opinion** (uh PIN yun) *noun* An idea that a person believes. An opinion cannot be proved true, and others may disagree with it. *Sandy's opinion is that it is more fun to play tennis than basketball.*

**plural** (PLUR ul) *noun, adjective* A noun that names more than one person, place, or thing. Most plurals are formed by adding the ending s or es. *Examples of plural nouns: foxes, clouds, kittens, teeth.*

**pourquoi tale** (por KWAH tayl) *noun* An old story that tells how something in nature came to be. *We read a pourquoi tale about how the elephant got its trunk.*

**prefix** (PREE fiks) *noun* A word part added before a word to change its meaning. *Examples: retell, undo, nonfiction.*

**proofread** (PROOF reed) *verb* To read a final copy of a written work carefully, in order to find and fix mistakes in spelling, capital letters, and punctuation.

**publish** (PUB lish) *verb* To share a final, correct copy of a written work with readers.

**quotation marks** (KWOH tay shun marks) *noun* The punctuation marks (" ") that show where a speaker's exact words begin and end.

**revise** (rih VIZE) *verb* To make changes to the draft of a written work. *Some writers revise their stories dozens of times to make the stories better and better.*

**sequence** (SEE kwins) *noun* The time order in which things happen. *Give the sequence of events in the story by telling what happens in the beginning, the middle, and the end.*

**singular** (SING gyuh lur) *adjective* Of a noun that names just one person, place, or thing. *Examples of singular nouns: fox, cloud, kitten, tooth.*

**suffix** (SUF iks) *noun* A word part added after a word to change its meaning or change the way it is used in a sentence. *Examples: swimmer, loudly, careful.*

**synonym** (SIN uh nim) *noun* A word with a similar meaning. *The words small and little are synonyms.*

**verb** *noun* A word that shows action or shows what something is. *Examples: Birds fly. Insects buzz. The cat naps. We are happy.*

# More Language Arts Words I Need to Know:

_____

_____

_____

_____

_____

_____

_____

# Important History Words I Need to Know!

**ancient** (AYN shunt) *adjective* Of the long-ago past.

**archaeology** (ar kee OL uh jee) *noun* The study of human ways of life long ago. The methods of archaeology involve careful digging in areas where people once lived.

**architecture** (AR kih tek chur) *noun* **1.** The designing of buildings. **2.** The buildings of a particular time or place. *The architecture of modern cities includes tall glass buildings.*

**century** (SEN chur ee) *noun* A period of 100 years. *The eighteenth century began in the year 1700.*

**civilization** (siv il ih ZAY shun) *noun* An organized society of people who build cities, have a political system, and develop the arts. *Sculpture was an advanced art during the civilization of ancient Greece.*

**colonist** (KOL uh nist) *noun* A person living in a land governed by a faraway country.

**culture** (KUL chur) *noun* The beliefs, customs, and arts of a people. *Pop music is a part of American culture.*

**custom** (KUS tum) *noun* A way of behaving that is shared by the members of a nation or group. *The customs of Vietnam include showing respect to elders.*

**decade** (DEK ayd) *noun* A period of ten years.

**explorer** (ik SPLOR ur) *noun* A person who travels through an area to learn about it.

**festival** (FES tuh vul) *noun* A time for celebrating and feasting, often linked to a religious event.

**folktale** (FOHK tayl) *noun* A story without an author, first told long ago and passed down through the years. *"Jack and the Beanstalk" is a folktale.*

**historian** (his TOR ee un) *noun* A person with special training who studies the events of the past and writes and teaches about them.

**human rights** (HYOO mun rites) *plural noun* The basic freedoms that belong to all people. Human rights include the right to live where and how one wishes, the right to a fair trial, the right to worship as one wishes, and the right to speak one's opinions.

**Independence Day** (in duh PEN dins day) *noun* The U.S. holiday held July 4, to celebrate the signing of the Declaration of Independence in 1776.

**Memorial Day** (muh MOR ee ul day) *noun* The U.S. holiday, observed on the last Monday in May, to honor the members of the armed forces who gave their lives in service to their country.

**monument** (MON yuh mint) *noun* A building, statue, or other structure put up to remember an important person, event, or idea.

**myth** (mith) *noun* An ancient story that tells about gods, goddesses, heroes, and magical events. *The Greek god Zeus plays a role in many myths.*

**native** (NAY tiv) adjective **1.** Of the first people to live in an area. *Native Americans lived in the United States long before Europeans arrived.* **2.** Of the land of one's birth.

**settlement** (SET ul mint) *noun* **1.** A place in which people new to an area have built homes. **2.** A small group of people living together.

# More History Words I Need to Know:

_____

_____

_____

_____

_____

_____

_____

_____

_____

_____

_____

_____

_____

_____

_____

_____

_____

_____

# Important Geography Words I Need to Know!

**capital** (KAP ih tul) *noun* A city that is the center of government of a state or a country.

**cliff** (klif) *noun* A high, steep, rocky slope that usually overlooks a large body of water.

**climate** (KLY mit) *noun* The temperatures, rainfall, and other weather conditions that a region usually has. *The climate near the North Pole includes long, harsh winters and short, cool summers.*

**coastal** (KOH stul) *adjective* Of or near the seashore.

**continent** (KON tih nint) *noun* One of the seven large land masses on the Earth's surface.

**county** (KOUN tee) *noun* An area within a state that has its own government for certain activities. *The county jail is run by a sheriff.*

**crop** (krop) *noun* A plant that people grow for food or other products.

**desert** (DEZ urt) *noun* A land that gets little rainfall.

**elevation** (el uh VAY shun) *noun* The height above sea level.

**environment** (in VY urn mint) *noun* The natural area in which plants, animals, and people live.

**grassland** (GRAS land) *noun* A land that gets enough rainfall to grow short or tall grasses. Some trees grow in a grassland, but most of the plants are low to the ground.

**harbor** (HAR bur) *noun* The part of a body of water that is near land, where ships stay when they are not out on the sea.

**kilometer** (KIL uh mee tur) or (kil OM ih tur) *noun* A measure of distance equal to 1,000 meters and about six-tenths of a mile.

**landform** *noun* A natural feature on the Earth's surface, such as a mountain, a valley, and a canyon.

**local** (LO kul) *adjective* Having to do with activities that are near a known place, such as a home neighborhood.

**mesa** (MAY suh) *noun* A high area of land with steep sides. The word *mesa* is Spanish for "table," and mesas look like tabletops.

**mountain pass** (MOUN tun pas) *noun* A narrow gap between mountains that allows travel from one side of a mountain range to the other.

**natural resource** (NACH ur ul REE sors) *noun* Something provided by nature and used by people. *Wood, coal, and water are natural resources.*

**North America** (north uh MEH rih kuh) *noun* One of the seven continents on the Earth. North America includes Canada, the United States, Mexico, Central America, the islands of the Caribbean Sea, and the island of Greenland in the northern Atlantic Ocean.

**plain** (playn) *noun* A large area of mainly flat land with few trees. A vast area of central North America is called the Great Plains.

**port** *noun* **1.** A place on a body of water where ships can load and unload their goods. **2.** A safe place for ships to wait; a harbor.

**scale** (skayl) *noun* A measuring tool on a map that shows inches or centimeters standing for distances on the Earth's surface. *The scale of distance on the map shows that one inch stands for a distance of 100 miles.*

**tide** *noun* The daily rise and fall of ocean waters. A high tide and a low tide occur about every twelve hours.

**valley** (VAL ee) *noun* A long, low area of land. Rivers often run through valleys.

**weather** (WETH ur) *noun* Temperature, clouds, wind, rain, and other conditions related to the layers of air above the earth's surface in a particular place and time.

# More Geography Words I Need to Know:

_____

_____

_____

_____

_____

_____

_____

_____

_____

_____

_____

_____

# Important Civics and Economics Words I Need to Know!

**authority** (uh THOR uh tee) *noun* Power to control others that belongs to a person or a group. *The police have the authority to make arrests.*

**barter** (BAR tur) *noun* To make a direct trade of products or services.

**budget** (BUJ it) *noun* A plan that shows how money will be spent over a certain time period. *verb* To make a budget.

**citizenship** (SIT ih zin ship) *noun* **1.** The state of being a citizen of a country. **2.** The responsibilities of a citizen.

**civic responsibility** (SIV ik rih spon suh BIL ih tee) *noun* The duty of a citizen or member of a community or country. *Helping to keep a neighborhood safe is a civic responsibility.*

**civil rights** (SIV il rites) *plural noun* Equal treatment under the law and other rights of citizens.

**common good** (KOM un good) *noun* The good effects for all when people join to form a community.

**consumer** (kun SOO mur) *noun* Someone who buys and uses products and services.

**currency** (KUR un see) *noun* The unit of money used in a country. *Coins and paper bills are forms of currency.*

**direct democracy** (dih REKT dih MOK ruh see) *noun* A form of self-government in which citizens serve as their own lawmakers. *Government by town meeting is a direct democracy.*

**duty** (DOO tee) *noun* An action that someone is supposed to do; a responsibility.

**economy** (ih KON uh mee) *noun* All of the activities connected to producing and consuming goods and services in a country or other place.

**exchange** (iks CHAYNJ) *verb* To make a trade.

**export** (EKS port) *noun* A product that is made in one country and sent to consumers in another country. *verb* To export products by sending them out of a country.

**federal** (FED uh rul) *adjective* Of a central government created by states that joined together.

**illegal** (ih LEE gul) *adjective* Against the law.

**import** (IM port) *noun* A product that is made in another country and used by consumers in the receiving country. *verb* To import products sent by another country.

**income** (IN kum) *noun* Money that is received. *People's paychecks are their source of income.*

**industry** (IN duh stree) *noun* The businesses involved in making certain kinds of goods or providing services, such as manufacturing or tourism.

**justice** (JUS tis) *noun* Fair treatment according to laws or ideas of fairness.

**legal** (LEE gul) *adjective* **1.** Allowed by law. **2.** Having to do with laws and lawmakers.

**legislature** (LEJ ih slay chur) *noun* The body of lawmakers in the government of a country or state. *The U.S. Congress is the national legislature.*

**manufacturing** (man yuh FAK chur ing) *noun* The making of products in

Words Every Third Grader Needs to Know!

factories.

**office** (OF is) *noun* **1.** A position of responsibility. *A governor holds the highest office in the state.* **2.** A department or agency of the U.S. government. *The Government Printing Office publishes documents.*

**producer** (pruh DOO sur) *noun* A person or business that makes a product or provides a service.

**profit** (PROF it) *noun* The money that a business has left after expenses are paid.

**public service** (PUB lik SUR vis) *noun* The work of providing the public with health, safety, transportation, education, and other services.

**represent** (REP rih zent) *noun* To act for others. *Elected lawmakers represent the people from their district or state.*

**representative democracy** (rep rih ZENT uh tiv dih MOK ruh see) *noun* A form of self-government in which citizens elect leaders and lawmakers who will take actions for them.

**tolerance** (TOL uh rens) *noun* Respect for the beliefs and practices of others when they are different from one's own.

# More Civics and Economics Words I Need to Know:

_____

_____

_____

_____

_____

_____

_____

_____

_____

_____

_____

_____

# Important Art Words I Need to Know!

**animation** (an ih MAY shun) *noun* The drawing of shapes in a series so that the shapes appear to be moving. *Movies with cartoon characters show the art of animation.*

**ballet** (ba LAY) *noun* A form of dance with particular positions, steps, leaps, and spins. Women ballet dancers perform many moves on the tips of their toes.

**chord** (kord) *noun* Two or more musical notes played at the same time.

**chorus** (KOR us) *noun* A group of people who sing together.

**cityscape** (SIT ee skayp) *noun* A painting, drawing, or photograph that shows a scene of a city or town.

**concert** (KON surt) *noun* A musical performance.

**cool colors** (kool KUL urz) *plural noun* Greens, blues, and purples. Cool colors suggest places and things that have cool temperatures.

**duet** (doo ET) *noun* A song or piece of music for two voices or instruments.

**horizontal** (hor ih ZON tul) *adjective* Of a line or shape that goes left and right. *Cross the letter* t *with a horizontal line.*

**landscape** (LAND skayp) *noun* A painting, drawing, or photograph that shows an outdoor scene, usually of nature.

**melody** (MEL uh dee) *noun* The series of musical notes that work together and have a rhythm. A song or part of a song has a melody.

**performance** (pur FOR muns) *noun* A work of music or dance, a play, or another work of art that is shown to an audience.

**position** (puh ZISH un) *noun* The way in which something, such as a body part, is placed. *Dancers learn basic positions of the feet.*

**quartet** (kwor TET) *noun* **1.** A group of four singers or musicians. **2.** A musical piece written for four voices or instruments.

**seascape** (SEE skayp) *noun* A painting, drawing, or photograph that shows a scene of an ocean, a coast, or a lake.

**still life** *noun* A painting, drawing, or photograph of objects arranged in a certain way. Fruit and glass objects are common subjects in still lifes.

**tempo** (TEM poh) *noun* The speed at which music is performed.

**trio** (TREE oh) *noun* **1.** A group of three singers or musicians. **2.** A musical piece written for three voices or instruments.

**vertical** (VUR tih kul) *adjective* Of a line or shape that goes up and down. *A tall building is a vertical shape.*

**warm colors** (warm KUL urz) *plural noun* Reds, oranges, and yellows. Warm colors suggest fire and other warm things.

# More Art Words I Need to Know:

_____

_____

_____

_____

_____

_____

_____

_____

_____

_____

_____

_____

_____

_____

_____

_____

_____

_____

_____

# Notes

# Answer Key

## Math

### Page 6
Students use this page to assess their own knowledge of the term *line segment*. Encourage students to explain how their drawing helps them remember the meaning of the term.

### Page 7
Sample responses for web:
Tools: ruler, scale, tape measure, measuring cup
Kinds: length, distance, weight, height, inches, meters, pounds, liters, miles, teaspoon
Activities: baking or cooking, hanging a picture, comparing heaviness, building a house
Importance: tells how far or how big something is, builds things so that they aren't lopsided
*Word Alert!* the suffix -ment

### Page 8
1. perimeter; area; drawing shows a square with each side 1 mile; 2. perimeter; area; drawing shows a square with each side 3 feet and 9 squares inside; 3. area, perimeter; drawing shows rectangle marked 3 inches by 5 inches, with 15 squares inside.

### Page 9
1. perpendicular; 2. diagonal; 3. Diagonal; 4. perpendicular; 5. diagonal
Sample responses: 6. chair seat and legs; 7. slanted bookcase

### Page 10
1. 357, 5 circled 2. $10.52, decimal point circled
3. Sample response: 15.64 4. They become larger.
Sample response: In 333, the 3 at the left stands for 300, which is larger than 30 or 3.
*Look It Up!* 1. a number; 2. a finger

### Page 11
1. A; 2. A; 3. A; 4. A; 5. B
Second activity: $\frac{1}{2}$, numerator/denominator labeled

### Page 12
1. B; 2. A; 3. B

### Page 13
Students' reasons will vary.
1. Yes, a product is the answer to a multiplication problem.
2. No, multiplication is like addition.
3. Yes, $2 \times 6 = 12$.
4. No, $6 \times 6 = 36$.
5. No, it's bigger because it is that number times another.

### Page 14
1. $15 \div 3$, $\frac{2}{5}$, $4\overline{)20}$
2. Students' drawings should show 7 grapes divided into 3 groups, with 1 leftover grape labeled *remainder*.

3. Sample response: You have 14 things to put into 3 groups. You can make 4 equal groups of 3, but 2 are left over.
*Challenge!* Sample response: A total is separated into parts, and the quotient tells how many equal parts there are.

### Page 15
1. pentagon; 2. rectangle; 3. octagon; 4. hexagon
Second activity: Yes, a triangle is a polygon because it has 3 connected line segments.

### Page 16
1. division, multiplication; 2. measurement, rectangle; 3. denominator, decimal point; 4. right triangle, angle; 5. perimeter, equilateral triangle
Second activity: Students' drawings should show an equilateral triangle with each side labeled 3 units.

### Page 17
1. quotient; 2. hexagon; 3. polygons; 4. multiples; 5. product; 6. fraction
Answer to message: You must be an expert!

### Page 18
Answers spell *figure*.

## Science and Health

### Page 20
Students use this page to assess their own knowledge of *nutrient*. Encourage students to explain how their drawing helps them remember word meaning.

### Page 21
Sample responses for web:
What: a body part or a behavior that helps a living thing survive
Why: plant or animal needs it to stay alive
Plants: roots that take in water, leaves that take in sunlight
Animals: fur for warmth, sharp claws for hunting
*Word Alert!* 1. adaptation; 2. adapt

### Page 22
Sample responses:
1. dodo birds, dinosaurs
2. They can't adapt to a changed environment. People hunt them until they die off.
3. Dead plants may have left seeds that grow into new plants, but extinct plants are not growing anywhere.
4. Scientists count the ones that are left. If there aren't enough, they might become extinct.
*Word Alert!* 1. extinction; 2. extinct

# Answer Key

## Page 23
1. carnivores; 2. herbivores; 3. carnivores;
4. herbivores; 5. carnivores
*Challenge!* Responses should show that herbivores eat plants, carnivores eat meat, and omnivores eat both.

## Page 24
1. spider–predator; insects–prey
2. deer–prey; wolves–predators
3. robin–predator; earthworm–prey
4. polar bear–predator; seal–prey
5. sharks–prey; seals–predators

## Page 25
1. A; 2. B; 3. B; 4. A; 5. A

## Page 26
1. reproduce; 2. habitat; 3. food web; 4. species;
5. reproduce; 6. food web

## Page 27
1. gas; 2. liquid; 3. liquid; 4. solid; 5. gas; 6. solid
*Look It Up!* Definitions will vary. Sample responses: A matter to discuss is an idea or problem. A state of matter is solid, liquid, or gas.

## Page 28
Students should label the whole diagram with *water cycle*, the rising arrows with *evaporate*, the full cloud with *condense*, and the rain with *precipitation*.

## Page 29
Sample responses:
1. water; 2. perspire; 3. sweat forms; 4. holds a lot of; 5. drink water

## Page 30
1. orbit; 2. tilts; 3. revolves; 4. axis.

## Page 31
Students' reasons will vary.
1. No, it is an icy body with an oval orbit. (Or) Yes, it is a body that orbits the Sun.
2. No, the Earth is part of the solar system.
3. Yes, though the moons also orbit their planets.
4. No, astronomers study space from the Earth.
5. No, an asteroid doesn't orbit a planet.
*Look It Up!* astronaut, asterisk, astronomy

## Page 32
1. decomposers, matter; 2. water vapor, condense;
3. adaptation, extinct; 4. orbit, solar system; 5. nutrients, reproduce
Second activity: Students' sentences will vary.

## Page 33
Answers spell *energy*.

## Page 34
1. precipitation; 2. producers; 3. astronomer;
4. predators; 5. axis; 6. ecosystem; 7. food web;
8. species

# Technology

## Page 36
Students use this page to assess their own knowledge of *force*. Encourage students to explain how their drawing helps them remember word meaning.

## Page 37
Sample responses for chart:
1. trying to think of as many ideas as you can, usually by talking with others
2. It's as if there's a high-energy storm in your brain.
3. You are getting ideas from other people, not just yourself. It's a fast kind of thinking.
4. They choose an idea to think about more slowly.

## Page 38
Sample responses:
1. ...you make final versions.
2. ...how well it worked.
3. ...a design is drawn, and a model is built.
4. ...work as well as people hope.
*Look It Up!* Definitions will vary.

## Page 39
Sample responses:
1. inventor; 2. inventor; 3. engineers; 4. engineers; 5. inventors, engineers
**Challenge!** Sample response: Long ago, an engine was any clever idea for solving problems, and an engineer was the person who thought of it.

## Page 40
Sample responses:
1. use e-mail and go to Web sites.
2. finds and displays the Web site with that address.
3. a colored link, the browser finds and displays a different Web page.
4. visit a Web site made by someone in Africa.
5. (name of browser used in school)
*Word Alert!* <u>Inter</u>net, <u>inter</u>active, <u>inter</u>connected
Sample response: Computer users linked in networks can play games together. Their screens change depending on their actions.

# Answer Key

## Page 41
Students' reasons will vary.
1. No, a ramp has no moving parts.
2. No, it has many machines working together.
3. No, it moves a longer distance.
4. Yes, a ladder is shaped like a ramp, and climbing it is easier than climbing straight up.
5. Yes, you have to push it up.
Second activity: Sample caption: Pushing an object up or down the ramp is easier than lifting it up or down.

## Page 42
1. wheel and axle; 2. pulley; 3. gear
Second activity: 1. pulley; 2. gear; 3. wheel and axle

## Page 43
Sample responses:
1. plastic, metal, glass
2. Try to use a mug or a glass instead.
3. Give the clothing to someone who can use it. Cut up the clothing to use as rags.
*Word Alert!* 1. use again; 2. make something seem new again; 3. fill again

## Page 44
1. gears, engineers; 2. brainstorm, reduce; 3. inventor, model; 4. pulleys, simple machines; 5. browser, Internet
Second activity: Students' sentences will vary.

## Page 45
Answers spell *design*.

## Page 46
1. recycle; 2. force; 3. pulley; 4. wheel; 5. engineer; 6. inventor
Message: You win!

## Language Arts

### Page 48
Students use this page to assess their own knowledge of *inference*. Encourage students to explain how their drawing helps them remember word meaning.

### Page 49
Sample responses for web:
What is it? a word that describes someone or something
Place: hilly, rocky, sunny, haunted
Person: tall, skinny, angry, smart
Food: spicy, sweet, salty, icky
Pet: furry, friendly, cuddly, sleepy

### Page 50
Sample responses:
1. The haiku is about the sound of flowing water in a brook.
2. A
3. Dark clouds overhead
4. rain, a bird, the ocean
5. Responses will vary.

### Page 51
1. unwise: not wise
2. teacher: someone who teaches
3. reuse: to use again; re+use
4. quietly: in a way that is quiet; quiet + ly
5. un (prefix) + fair + ly (suffix)
6. A prefix is added before a word, and a suffix is added after.

### Page 52
1. synonyms; 2. antonyms; 3. antonyms; 4. synonyms; 5. synonyms; 6. antonyms; 7. antonyms; 8. synonyms
*Look It Up!* Sample response: The prefix ant- means "opposite," and antonyms have opposite meanings."

### Page 53
1. watched–verb; game–noun
2. dancers–noun; twirled–verb
3. cats–noun; stretch–verb; yawn–verb
4. mother–noun; is–verb; teacher–noun
5. house–noun; sits–verb; hill–noun
*Challenge!* Sample response: A verb is a thing, and a thing is a noun.

### Page 54
1. P; 2. P; 3. P; 4. S; 5. S; 6. S; 7. S; 8. P; 9. P; 10. P
*Challenge!* woman, dog, penny, glasses, chairs, houses, rabbits, bush, dress, wolf

### Page 55
1. facts; 2. facts; 3. opinions; 4. opinions; 5. facts
Second activity: Sample responses: 1. The Red Sox play baseball. 2. The Red Sox are sure to win the World Series this year.

### Page 56
1. Mama Mouse, Andy, and Allie
2. "Pizza!" He sounds excited.
3. Mama is speaking. The words are in the same paragraph with "said Mama."
Second activity: Responses will vary.

### Page 57
Wording of meanings will vary.
1. noisy and out of order; context clue
2. very cold; context clue
3. plant scientists; definition
4. fast sailing ships of long ago; definition
5. hate; context clue
*Word Alert!* Sample response: If you want to define a new word, look for its definition in a dictionary.

# Answer Key

## Page 58
Students' reasons will vary.
1. Yes, it comes from the author's imagination.
2. No, they're listed in alphabetical order.
3. Yes, it could give facts about butterflies.
4. No, nonfiction is true.
5. No, a fiction book doesn't have an index.
*Word Alert!* Sample response: Nonfiction is not fiction—it's true.

## Page 59
1. B; 2. A; 3. B; 4. A; 5. A

## Page 60
1. proofread; 2. draft; 3. sequence; 4. publish;
5. revise; 6. homophones
*Look It Up!* Drawings will vary but might show a draft of a written work, the effects of a draft of air, and a draft animal.

## Page 61
Answers spell *revise*.

## Page 62
1. homophones; 2. sequence; 3. synonyms;
4. suffix; 5. plural; 6. opinion
Riddle and answer: How is the letter k like flour?
(You can't make cake without it!)

## History

### Page 64
Students use this page to assess their own knowledge of the term *human rights*. Encourage students to explain how their drawing helps them remember the meaning of the term.

### Page 65
Sample responses for web:
What: someone who studies the past
Search for: old letters, old newspapers, objects that people used long ago, old photos
Where: at museums, in colleges, at historic sites, in the history department of a city or town
Importance: teach people about important events, understand what really happened long ago, help people understand their own times
Word Alert! A historian studies history. A librarian works in a library. A musician plays music.

### Page 66
Drawings and responses will vary.

### Page 67
1. century; 2. century; 3. decade; 4. decade;
5. century
*Look It Up!* Possible words include *cent, centimeter, centipede, centennial,* and *centigrade*.

### Page 68

1. Independence Day; 2. Memorial Day; 3. Memorial Day; 4. Independence Day; 5. Memorial Day
*Word Alert!* Underline <u>commemorate</u>. Sample response: to remember and honor an event.

### Page 69
1. native; 2. explorers; 3. colonists; 4. settlement;
5. Explorers
*Word Alert!* 1. colonists; 2. explorers; 3. settle

### Page 70
Students' reasons will vary.
1. No, it's usually noisy and lively, with parades and crowds.
2. Yes, stories are passed down from parents to children over the years.
3. No, a myth is fiction, though it may have an adventure in it.
4. Yes, everyday people told the stories long ago.
5. Yes, people have religious practices, holidays, and ways of cooking and eating.

### Page 71
1. B; 2. A; 3. B; 4. A; 5. B
*Challenge!* Sample response: Today we know about the art, buildings, beliefs, and rulers of the large society of people who lived long ago in Mexico and Central America. They were called the Maya people. We know about them because of scientists who have dug up objects from buried cities.

### Page 72
1. historian, century; 2. monument, myth;
3. native, archaeology; 4. civilization, architecture;
5. festival, culture
Second activity: Sentences will vary.

### Page 73
1. ancient; 2. customs; 3. explorer; 4. folktale;
5. colonist; 6. rights; 7. decade
Answer to riddle: a sponge!

### Page 74
Answers spell *happen*.

## Geography
### Page 76
Students use this page to assess their own knowledge of *environment*. Encourage students to explain how their drawing helps them remember word meaning.

### Page 77
1. weather; 2. climate; 3. climate; 4. climate;
5. weather; 6. climate; 7. weather; 8. weather
Second activity: Sample response: The weather is very hot and mostly dry in summer, with afternoon thunderstorms. It is chilly and dry in winter.

# Answer Key

## Page 78
1. grasslands; 2. desert; 3. deserts; 4. grasslands; 5. desert; 6. desert
*Word Alert!* Sample response: A grassland is a land in which grass is the main plant.

## Page 79
1. B; 2. A; 3. A; 4. B; 5. A
*Look It Up!* Sample responses: 1. compare weights; 2. measure distances on a map; 3. are its outer layer

## Page 80
*Continents*: Asia, North America, Europe, Antarctica, Australia, South America, Africa
*North America*: Canada, Greenland, United States, Mexico, Caribbean islands, Central America

## Page 81
Sample responses:
1. from nature; 2. build or power; 3. wheat, rice; 4. are not farmed; 5. water
Second activity: 1. crops; 2. natural resources

## Page 82
1. B; 2. A; 3. B; 4. A; 5. A
*Challenge!* Yes, the same city could be the capital for the state and the center of government for its own county.

## Page 83
Students' reasons will vary.
1. No, sea level is at an elevation of 0.
2. No, a valley could be formed by a river that is far from a mountain.
3. Yes, it's a way to pass through land.
4. Yes, a river valley may have rich soil for farming.
*Word Alert!* An elevated train runs on tracks above the ground.

## Page 84
1. cliff; 2. mesa; 3. landforms; 4. cliff; 5. mesa
*Word Alert!* plain; An airplane flew over flat land.

## Page 85
1. A; 2. A; 3. B; 4. A; 5. A; 6. A

## Page 86
1. kilometers, elevation; 2. climate, coastal; 3. local, environment; 4. natural resource, grassland; 5. landform, continent; 6. weather, crops
Second activity: Sentences will vary.

## Page 87
Answers spell *desert*.

## Page 88
1. continents; 2. weather; 3. kilometer; 4. coastal; 5. elevation; 6. plain; 7. crops; 8. valley

# Civics and Economics

## Page 90
Students use this page to assess their own knowledge of *justice*. Encourage students to explain how their drawing helps them remember word meaning.

## Page 91
Sample responses for web:
What: showing respect for other people's beliefs and behaviors
Importance: People get along better. They treat each other fairly. They don't force others to act a certain way.
How shown by government: No laws force people to go to a particular church. People aren't punished for believing as they wish.
Opposite: prejudice, hatred, intolerance

## Page 92
1. illegal; 2. legal; 3. legal; 4. legal; 5. illegal; 6. illegal
*Word Alert!* 1. not legal; 2. not perfect; 3. not complete

## Page 93
1. import; 2. exported; 3. import; 4. imported; 5. exports
*Challenge!* Students' drawings may show arrows or a scale to suggest a balanced number of imports and exports.

## Page 94
1. Sample response: teachers and dentists
2. Sample response: shoes, furniture
3. customer
4. Sample response: ... like their products and buy more of them.
5. Sample response: Workers who produce things are consumers whenever they buy things.

## Page 95
Sample responses:
1. ...that a school office is a room, but an office that someone holds is a position.
2. ...the principal and teachers.
3. ...make decisions and vote on laws in ways that will help the voters.
4. ...to tell the office holder about a problem they would like him or her to solve, like fixing roads.
*Word Alert!* office, official, officers

## Page 96
1. A; 2. A; 3. A; 4. A; 5. B; 6. A

## Page 97
Sample responses:
1. buses and subways; 2. police officers; 3. benefits; 4. should work; 5. sanitation; 6. pay for

# Answer Key

## Page 98
**1.** B; **2.** A; **3.** B; **4.** A; **5.** A; **6.** B

## Page 99
**1.** currency; **2.** economy; **3.** barter; **4.** exchange;
**5.** exchange
*Look It Up!* Provide students with an advanced dictionary for this activity.

## Page 100
Students' reasons will vary.
**1.** Yes, human rights belong to all people, and civil rights belong to citizens.
**2.** Yes, we have to go to school and obey laws.
**3.** Yes, taxpayers obey the law.
**4.** No, civil rights have to do with fairness and justice.
**5.** No, every country grants citizenship to people who were born there or who become citizens there.

## Page 101
Sample responses:
**1.** ...elect lawmakers who will govern them.
**2.** ...the state government to obey the national law.
**3.** ...on laws about taxes, education, other public services, war, and other matters.
**4.** ...share their views and vote the way they would if they were making laws.
**5.** ...where and how would millions of people meet to discuss the issues? Direct democracy could only work for small communities.

## Page 102
**1.** exports, economy; **2.** federal, budget;
**3.** authority, justice; **4.** represent, common good; **5.** illegal, legislature
Second activity: Sentences will vary.

## Page 103
Answers spell *profit*.

## Page 104
**1.** tolerance; **2.** consumer; **3.** civil; **4.** citizenship;
**5.** legal; **6.** legislature
Riddle and answer: The more you take from it, the bigger it gets. What is it? (a hole)

## The Arts
## Page 106
Students use this page to assess their own knowledge of *animation*. Encourage students to explain how their drawing helps them remember word meaning.

## Page 107
Sample responses for web:
What: a show of a work of art for an audience
Kinds: music, dance, comedy, drama, gymnastics

Describing words: exciting, lively, suspenseful, entertaining, funny
Why important: Share good times; appreciate beauty; admire skill; enjoy music; enter a new world

## Page 108
**1.** label long bar *vertical* and crossed bar *horizontal*
**2.** E
**3.** Sample responses: windowsill, top of desk
**4.** Sample responses: flagpole, long side of door
**5.** Drawings will vary.
*Look It Up!* Sample response: The horizon is the horizontal line between sky and water or sky and land.

## Page 109
**1.** warm color; **2.** warm color; **3.** cool color; **4.** cool color; **5.** cool color; **6.** warm color; **7.** warm color;
**8.** cool color

## Page 110
Sample responses:
**1.** arms; **2.** balance; **3.** leaps; **4.** one leg; **5.** to the music
*Challenge!* Possible answers include arabesque, en pointe, jeté, pas de deux.

## Page 111
**1.** A; **2.** A; **3.** B; **4.** A; **5.** B
*Word Alert!* They all name things with three parts or members.

## Page 112
**1.** still life; **2.** seascape; **3.** cityscape; **4.** landscape;
**5.** landscape (or seascape)
*Challenge!* Pictures will vary.

## Page 113
Students' reasons will vary.
**1.** No, a chorus is a group.
**2.** No, you can't hum more than one note at a time.
**3.** No, a melody is made of notes.
**4.** Yes, a tempo can be fast, slow, or in-between.
**5.** Yes, a concert is a musical performance.

## Page 114
**1.** animation, position; **2.** ballet, tempo; **3.** vertical, landscape; **4.** quartet, concert; **5.** chorus, duet
Second activity: Sentences will vary.

## Page 115
Answers spell *beauty*.

## Page 116
**1.** warm; **2.** trio; **3.** animation; **4.** chorus;
**5.** performance; **6.** vertical; **7.** seascape; **8.** position

fiction

noun

synonym

antonym

nonfiction

suffix

simple machine

inference

prefix

*noun* A story that is made up by the author.

*noun* A word that names a person, place, or thing.

*noun* A word with a similar meaning.

*noun* A word with an opposite meaning.

*noun* A true story or other written work that gives information. Nonfiction is about things that really happened and does not come from the author's imagination. Science books, history books, and biographies are examples of nonfiction.

*noun* A word part added after a word to change its meaning or change the way it is used in a sentence.

*noun* One of the six basic machines that are used alone or as part of other machines to make work easier. Simple machines have no or few moving parts. The six simple machines are the ramp, pulley, wheel and axle, gear, wedge, lever, and screw.

*noun* An idea that a reader can figure out even though it is not directly stated by the author.

*noun* A word part added before a word to change its meaning.

| | | |
|---|---|---|
| History<br><br>**century** | History<br><br>**settlement** | Geography<br><br>**continent** |
| History<br><br>**ancient** | History<br><br>**culture** | Geography<br><br>**climate** |
| Language Arts<br><br>**verb** | History<br><br>**civilization** | Geography<br><br>**capital** |

noun A period of 100 years.

adjective Of the long-ago past.

noun A word that shows action or shows what something is.

noun 1. A place in which people new to an area have built homes. 2. A small group of people living together.

noun The beliefs, customs, and arts of a people.

noun An organized society of people who build cities, have a political system, and develop the arts.

noun One of the seven large land masses on the Earth's surface.

noun The temperatures, rainfall, and other weather conditions that a region usually has.

noun A city that is the center of government of a state or a country.

| Geography | Geography | Civics and Economics |
|---|---|---|
| **environment** | **North America** | **consumer** |

| Geography | Geography | Civics and Economics |
|---|---|---|
| **desert** | **natural resource** | **citizenship** |

| Geography | Geography | Civics and Economics |
|---|---|---|
| **crop** | **landform** | **budget** |

noun The natural area in which plants, animals, and people live.

noun A land that gets little rainfall.

noun A plant that people grow for food or other products.

noun One of the seven continents on the Earth. North America includes Canada, the United States, Mexico, Central America, the islands of the Caribbean Sea, and the island of Greenland in the northern Atlantic Ocean.

noun Something provided by nature and used by people.

noun A natural feature on the Earth's surface, such as a mountain, a valley, and a canyon.

noun Someone who buys and uses products and services.

noun 1. The state of being a citizen of a country. 2. The responsibilities of a citizen.

noun A plan that shows how money will be spent over a certain time period. verb To make a budget.

**industry**

**concert**

**vertical**

**import**

**legislature**

**landscape**

**export**

**justice**

**horizontal**

noun The businesses involved in making certain kinds of goods or providing services, such as manufacturing or tourism.

noun A musical performance.

adjective Of a line or shape that goes up and down.

noun A product that is made in another country and used by consumers in the receiving country. verb To import products sent by another country.

noun The body of lawmakers in the government of a country or state.

noun A painting, drawing, or photograph that shows an outdoor scene, usually of nature.

noun A product that is made in one country and sent to consumers in another country. verb To export products by sending them out of a country.

noun Fair treatment according to laws or ideas of fairness.

adjective Of a line or shape that goes left and right.

| Math | Math | Math |
| --- | --- | --- |
| **angle** | **digit** | **division** |

| Math | Math | Math |
| --- | --- | --- |
| **fraction** | **multiplication** | **remainder** |

| Science and Health | Science and Health | Science and Health |
| --- | --- | --- |
| **decomposer** | **ecosystem** | **food web** |

noun Figuring out how many times one amount can fit into another amount.

noun The number left over when a number is not divided evenly.

noun The network of connections among plants, animals that eat plants, and animals that eat plant-eaters.

noun One of the numbers 0 through 9.

noun Adding a number to itself two or more times.

noun A community of living things along with the nonliving things in a natural area.

noun The space between two lines that meet at an endpoint, or the space between two flat surfaces that meet at a line.

noun A part of a whole.

noun A life form that breaks down the remains of dead plants and animals into simple nutrients that return to the soil to nourish plants.

| Science and Health | Science and Health | Technology |
|---|---|---|
| **nutrient** | **revolve** | **recycle** |
| Science and Health | Science and Health | Technology |
| **matter** | **precipitation** | **inventor** |
| Science and Health | Science and Health | Technology |
| **habitat** | **orbit** | **engineer** |

noun A substance that nourishes, or feeds, living things.

noun Anything that can be weighed and takes up space.

noun The natural area in which a plant or an animal lives.

verb To take a circular path around a central object.

noun A form of water that falls to the Earth's surface. Rain, hail, snow, and sleet are precipitation.

noun The path that a planet or other body takes around a star, or the path that a moon takes around its planet.
verb To take a path around a body in space.

verb To take out useful materials from things that are thrown away and find new uses for those materials.

noun Someone who uses science and imagination to plan something that has never been made before.

noun A person who uses science to design, plan, and build machines, buildings, products, and other technologies.